I'm Here to Change the World

Copyright © 2025 California Poets in the Schools

All rights reserved. No part of this book may be reproduced, stored in a retrieval system, or transmitted in any form, by any means, electronic, mechanical, photocopying, recording or otherwise, except by a reviewer who may quote brief passages in a review. Please notify California Poets in the Schools or the authors when using quoted "fair use" embodied in articles and reviews and for not-for-profit education or personal growth purposes. Your support of the authors' copyright is appreciated.

First Edition.
Paperback ISBN # 978-0-939927-34-0

The book's title, *I'm Here to Change the World*, comes from a poem within this anthology with the same title, written by Allison Sullivan from Marin County.

Cover art: Vida Pringle, 8th Grade, Sonoma County

California Poets in the Schools
415-221-4201
info@cpits.org
https://www.californiapoets.org

Meg Hamill, Executive Director
David Sibbet, President of the Board

I'm Here to Change the World

2024-25
California Poets in the Schools
Statewide Anthology

*In memory of Tobey Kaplan,
who believed deeply in the power of poetry
to transform young lives.*

Foreword

At California Poets in the Schools, we hold fast to our vision: that every young person in California should have the opportunity to discover their unique voice and use it to speak their truth. Today, this mission feels more urgent than ever—and worth protecting.

Young people today face extraordinary challenges. Across California, they carry the weight of climate change, as many communities have endured devastating wildfires that bring trauma to entire regions. Students must prepare for the possibility of gun violence in their schools, rehearsing how to hide in silence behind a barricaded door. Screen culture and the pull of social media fragment attention, while the number of young people who read for pleasure continues to decline. Too many encounter harrowing racial profiling in their daily lives.

Poetry offers solace and hope. It also offers truth-telling — the courage to name what is difficult, and the vision to imagine what could be. Young people have always turned to poetry in times of uncertainty: to grieve, to question, to celebrate, and to envision a different future. This anthology continues that tradition.

And in this era of shrinking arts funding, it is vital to remember that behind each poem stands a Poet-Teacher and a classroom teacher who placed value on the act of writing poetry. They created the space, encouragement, and guidance that allow youth voices to be nurtured and heard.

The students in this anthology are doing something powerful. First, they are creating. To create is to resist the constant pull of consumerism. Instead of only absorbing content, they are making something new. In poetry classes, students practice the art of creating something from nothing — an essential human skill. Just as importantly, they are raising their voices. Through this publication, their words reach beyond the classroom and the family circle, often for the very first time. The poems in these pages remind us that young people are not only preparing for the future — they are shaping it now, showing us how to see, feel, and understand our world.

This anthology is a gift from young people to their communities. Welcome it. Celebrate them. Share their gift with others. And above all, let these poems remind us that even in difficult times, hope and imagination endure — and that young people will continue to discover their voices, speak their truths, and thrive.

Meg Hamill
Executive Director
California Poets in the Schools

Table of Contents

Foreword 5

Our Emotional Worlds 13
    Hope, Sadie Van Elderen 15
    Joy in My Heart, Elle Sloan 16
    Greed, Sophie Andersen 17
    Heart of Knowledge, Elliot Souza 18
    Pressure Pushing Down on Me, Margeaux Le Fey 19
    Joy – I Tried to Write About It..., Zion Adams 20
    Jealousy, Eve Chapman 21
    I Love My Joy, Aurora Crespin 22
    Joy Is the Best Feeling Ever, Sofia Piedrasanta 23
    Things That Make Me Happy, Leo Kostiner 24
    Darkness, Will Maynard 25
    Emptiness, Mina Ghandi 26
    Joy, Rory Dunlap 27

Writing Ourselves/Writing our Future 29
    I Am From Black History, Harmony Diggs 31
    carousel, Vee Lee 32
    Secrets of the World, Jack Gorman 33
    Not My Problem, Leah Frink 34
    Poetry Is, Tommy Schaufler 35
    Not From Here, Angel Ramirez 36
    Dead Ends, Kimimila (Kat) Iron Bull Sanchez 37
    Food and Family, Sophia Winchell 38
    Sopa de Gallina, Maycon Rivas 39
    From Cities to Woods, Cosmos MacLeod 40
    From a Ranch in the Mountains, Jesus Loya 41
    The Waves in Snow, Cian Fahey 42
    There's a Kind of Silence, Sylvester Hales 43
    I am Batman, Leonardo Lopez Martinez 44

Quiet Dawn, Luis Peña 45
My Life, Salvadoran Pupusas, Mia Arrazate 46
No Place, April Veloz 47
Is it Me?, Claudia Kenyon 48
Cliché, Lillian Dempewolf 49
After, Demetri Gai 50
I am Happy, Bowie O'Dell 51
Respect, Jose Vasquez Montero 52
I Like You, But I Don't Like You, Juanita Ramirez Alvarado 53
Untitled, Aubrey Koifman 54
Unmatched Love, Arianna Alcala 55
I Am, Diana Jaramillo 56
Face Caterpillar, Max O. Post-Leibe 57
The Same, Group Poem 59
I'm Here to Change the World, Allison Sullivan 60
This is Me, Georgia McEachern 61
You Can be Anything, Conor DeVore 62
I Am, Mac Flanigan 63
Me, Niya Frisella 64
My Writing, Alexandra Mohtashemi 65
Middle Child, Jacqueline Zamora Rodriguez 66
The Raging Sea, Siddhartha Arturo Sil 67
I Come From (Paiute, a Native American Tribe), Morgan Wilder 68

Imaginations 69
The Foxes, Nathan Castillo Vail 71
Parrot, Desmond Hanley 72
Under the Banyan Sky, Yael Shenassafar 74
The Door to My Imagination, Lala Mendez 75
Fractured Star, Athena Driesen 76
Recipe for Neon Rainbow Stars, Genesis Sanchez 77
Take Me Down to Earth, Cynthia Marsolan 78
Something Strange, Iris Riley 80
The Unsung Hero, Izzy Wells 81
How I Would Paint, Noora Sulem 83
Untitled, Lisa Zheng 84

Woman in the Water, Evelyn Allen 85
Maybe it Was, Amelie Lamy 86
Animal Alliteration, Group Poem 87
Poetry, Group Poem 88
The Door to My Imagination, Olivia DeMarco 90

The Natural World 91
Sunset, Romy Amash 93
What the Rain Told Me, Brodey Saeteurn 94
Our Beautiful Mother Earth, Kayla Hernandez 95
Our Amazing Oceans, Lya Uzri 96
My Special Place, Myles Pirtle 97
Our Oceans, Ben Kozubik 98
Elephants and Mice How Nice, Avery Chun 99
Three Haiku, Ava McCloud 100
If You Were a Butterfly Like Me, Ellie Marsh 101
Eagles Wolves Winter Stars and Rain They're All Related,
Cressida Maccubbin 102
Mother Earth's Feelings, Anthony Barajas 103
The Movingness, Liv Sarkovich 104
King of the Woods Beyond, Milena Barker 106
Mother of the Sea, Anna Neto 108
I Wish to Grow Like the Sea Wind, Axel Tripp 109
Grass, Ella Cha 110
My Thoughts on Our Oceans, Daniella Maloney Flores 111
Chime of the Wind, Micah Dunn 112
AXOLOTL, Siena Filian 113
Three Haiku, Ayden Marrufo-McCloud 114
The Hand of Nature, Charlotte Shaw 115
Hawk vs. Snake, Manuel Vielma 116
Dazzling Snakes, Carter Crosswell 117

Where We're at Now 119
The Growing Name, Jeriko Fleming 121
Three Haiku, Jeremiah Patrick 122
Erase My Birthright, Juno Phipps 124

Where the Moon Meets the Sun, the Sun Meets the Moon,
Jasmine Guerrero Sevilla 126
Skin, Athena Marino DeFrates 128
Untitled, Aurora Rocha 129
Brasil!, Lucy DeLaney 130
Please Don't Leave, Salisa Leon 131
Listen, Scarlett Fierro 132
The Fires, Esteban Solis... 133
Big Orange Flame, Jackson Gomez.. 134
In What Language Should I Speak to You?, Tess Belger 137
just friends, Madeline Meyers 139
None of us are Natives, Olivia Smith.. 140
Smack!, Viktor Azbill 141
A Girl's Only Option, Sayeh Shenassafar................................. 143
How Am I Supposed to Cry, Timothy Gene Southwick............ 145
One Sweet Dream, Kaedyn Comer.. 146
Three Haiku, Linkn Carver 147
It Would Be Easier if We Were Less Frail, Frej Barty 149
Enjoy It, Ava Desmond 150

Letters, Gifts & Odes 151
Ode to Life, Ginger DeWoody.. 153
I Am Giving You..., Malin Kunes... 154
Ode to Taylor Swift, Tatum Goldberg.. 156
A Letter from the Moon, Amara Berry 158
Dear Lovely Sky, Callie Marsh 160
Dear Poem, Sequoia Dervin... 161
Dear Vincent, Natalie Robins 163
Dear Stars and Skies, Valerie Zell 164
Dear Father Patrick, Jadon Castle-Haley.................................. 166
An Ode to the Small Things, Fintan O'Dwyer 167
Dear Mom..., Parker Budesa 168
Ode to Cold Things, Avalon Carrington 169
Ode to Black, Group Poem.. 170
Ode to Blue, Zack Mitchell 171
Midnight Black, Dylan Burke 172

Ode to Blue, William Jimenez 173
Green and Brown, the Perfect Pair, Emilia Rauschecker 174
Cobalt, Charles Sullivan 176
Whale & Butterfly, Lexi Lawton 177

Poet-Teacher Poems 179
Let Them Write, Dominic Rossi 184
Big Girl Panties, Michele Rivers 186
Ars Poetica—Bolinas, Virginia Barrett 188
Jostling with Gentrification, Johnnierenee Nia Nelson 189
Pearls, Alice Pero 190
Jackson's Nose, Brian R. Martens 192
Breadth of Being, Blake More 194
Dandelion Dictate, Dawn Trook 195
To Paint a Thing of Beauty, Lulu Wong 197
Spring Gifts, Claire Blotter 199
A Miner's Lament, Kirsten Casey 201

About California Poets in the Schools 202

Our Emotional Worlds

Hope

Hope is a graceful, fast sea otter shooting
like a furry little grey rocket up to the surface;
as water (agua) brushes her short, silky fur.

Hope is a school of salmon, bravely swimming
up the river, never knowing if they will end up
in a grizzly bear's mouth.

Hope will hop from seedling to seedling
making a perfect yellow/ green (verde) color
as she twirls through the air.

Hope is the glistening breath of the moon, (luna)
traveling through space to land
on an enchanting white flower.

Sadie Van Elderen, 4th Grade
Mountain View Elementary, Santa Barbara County
Katherine James, Classroom Teacher
Cie Gumucio, Poet-Teacher

Joy in My Heart

Joy is great. There is a heart in my joy.
There is thankfulness in my joy.
There are hearts inside of hearts in my joy.
There are strings of joy in my heart.
Joy is in my house. There are hands of joy
in my friends and me.

Elle Sloan, 2nd Grade
Park Elementary School, Marin County
Allison Ponce de Leon, Classroom Teacher
Claire Blotter, Poet-Teacher

Greed

Greed is a cicada split in two
Its shell still sings despite the rot
Infected, it hums beneath the trees
Its purpose unfinished
Left to clot
Massospora floods their brain
Replaces thought with raw desire
It dances while its kind collapse
Their wings consumed by a quiet fire
Blood lies still in crimson heaps
Their hollow body, twitching legs
The spores that burst like shattering eggs
Continuing to stain their land

Sophie Andersen, 11th Grade
Willits High School, Mendocino County
Katrina Hall, Classroom Teacher
Bill Churchill, Poet-Teacher

Heart of Knowledge

My heart is an infinite
vortex of unanswered
questions. Within my heart
I am constantly tormented
by the reality of the
universe and all of the
unknown wonders lingering
inside. My heart holds
the desire and yearning for
knowledge outside of human
grasp, waiting to be discovered,
the knowledge of unfathomable
depth. My heart will
forever be thirsty for
the void of knowledge.

Elliot Souza, 6th Grade
Hydesville Elementary School, Humboldt County
Lily MacMillan, Classroom Teacher
Dan Zev Levinson, Poet-Teacher

Pressure Pushing Down on Me

Pressure pushing on me
like two bricks. Wrapping around my
heart and waist like a
python. It screams, "No breaks."
In its dark robe with a spear
ready to strike your heart, soul
and mind. Ready to make you
work. Your suffering is its
power. Once it becomes the
biggest part of your soul, there is
no escape. No other feeling but
pressure.

Margeaux Le Fey, 3rd Grade
Arcata Elementary School, Humboldt County
Payton Irizarry, Classroom Teacher
Dan Zev Levinson, Poet-Teacher

Joy – I Tried to Write About It . . .

When pines shake out their hair to dry
I wonder if they realize what a pretty sound they make.
When water falls on tents and lakes, it's beautiful.
Hikes may just be a hint of honey, glazing joy with its sweet taste.

Then . . .

Death is nothing at all.
It does not count.
They have only slipped away into the next room.
Nothing has happened.

You may have slipped away and I'm still trying to forget you,
but the harder I try, the more I think about you.
I'm not sure if I'm holding on or just holding my breath.
All these things about loss and Chris are overwhelming.

I looked outside my window, and it was raining at
my little cousin's funeral.
I felt so much pain, I felt like I was getting choked by a chain.
This whole thing was driving me super insane.
There are no cures for tears. In my eyes all I saw was flares.
I loved my Vinny so much, but I know he is doing just fine above.

There is no joy.
Long after I have given up ...
My heart still searches for you without my permission.

Zion Adams, 6th Grade
San Jose Middle School, Marin County
Kaia Lauerman (née Pruett), Classroom Teacher
Michele Rivers, Poet-Teacher

Jealousy

Jealousy is a viper snake,
twisting around your neck.
It poisons your mind.
Your heart starts to drum a payback song.
Your fists start to clench,
your mouth goes dry,
your lips get chapped.
Jealousy crushes friendship.
Jealousy is a text message read with no response.
It's sour and bitter, leaving your eyes blurry with tears.
It's a cold slap in the face.
It's a thorn in your shoe you can't find.
You stay up late at night because of jealousy,
forming a corrupt plan.
No one knows how to get rid of it.
Some survive, but some are left
with the payback song in their hearts.

Eve Chapman, 6th Grade
Mill Valley Middle School, Marin County
Brenda Poletti, Classroom Teacher
Claire Blotter, Poet-Teacher

I Love My Joy

Joy is the beach where there are golden sands and the sapphire ocean.
I hear waves hit the rocks on shore.
I see crabs skedaddle across the sand.
The sun warms my skin.
I love the beach.

Joy is like finishing a good drawing.
Using vibrant colors like golden yellow and aqua blue.
I hear the taping of my pencil on the paper.
I love to draw.

Joy is touching my cat's fur, it's as soft as a feather.
His nose is a soft pink, wet and small.
After sitting in the sun his fur is warm when he sits on my lap.
I love my cat.

Joy is having a good education.
Spending time with the best teacher I could ever wish for.
I hear the laughter in the classroom, and kids playing and singing.
I love my school.

Aurora Crespin, 4th Grade
Lu Sutton Elementary, Marin County
Emma Parks, Classroom Teacher
Michele Rivers, Poet-Teacher

Joy Is the Best Feeling Ever

Joy is walking a sacred path through the trees,
as birds chirp sweetly, and winds softly tease.
Lush leaves sway gently in the warm, golden light,
while a waterfall sparkles, a sapphire in flight.

Joy is like a basketball game where anticipation grows,
dribbling the ball as excitement flows.
In slow motion, I shoot, heart racing so fast,
the ball goes in, and cheers fill the air.
Echoing the last.

Joy is a butterfly soaring into the blue,
or a shooting star's whisper—unseen, yet true.

Joy is like the canvas where colors collide,
creating a masterpiece, where my heart opens wide.

I feel full of joy with ice cream in hand, I savor each bite,
creamy and sweet, pure delight in the night.

In every small moment, joy's bliss I embrace,
The best feeling ever, love etched on my face.

Joy is the best feeling ever.

Sofia Piedrasanta, 4th grade
Lu Sutton Elementary, Marin County
Kimberly Navabpour, Classroom Teacher
Michele Rivers, Poet-Teacher

Things That Make Me Happy

Joy is walking in the mountains where my feet sink into the
snow like a big marshmallow with a soft crunch.
I hear nothing except for a slight breeze and my footsteps
echoing in the mountainside.
All I see is the white of the snow on the mountain,
the yellowness of the sun, and the blueness of the sky.

Joy is the baseball hitting my bat and flying into the outfield,
getting cheered on by my team as I run the bases.
I seem to fly over the players as I slide into the base.

Joy is playing with my dog; he jumps at me when we play fetch.
He drags me across the floor when we are playing tug-of-war.

Joy is being at school on the playground playing with my friends,
or sitting inside my classroom quietly learning poetry and
drawing when we have free time.

I feel full of joy when I'm eating warm,
delicious spaghetti and meatballs.
I love eating the soft pasta and savoring the warm meatballs
that have a tinge of garlic and a tinge of rosemary.

There is so much joy in the world, these are mine.

Leo Kostiner, 4th grade
Lu Sutton Elementary, Marin County
Kimberly Navabpour, Classroom Teacher
Michele Rivers, Poet-Teacher

Darkness

I see a bright bird locked in its cage.
I fall into a closed void every time I look at it.
I see hair strands that lasted for generations.
There is a new color in the picture,
it is called sadness.
It is fully painted in it.
It glows with solar flames.
It contains a nova of color
only I can see.
It is invisible,
because it is soaring
through a dark void.
It is lost in a forest at night
unable to escape,
because it was put in a jar
like a moonlit butterfly.

Will Maynard, 4th Grade
Edna Maguire Elementary School, Marin County
Jessica Tran, Classroom Teacher
Claire Blotter, Poet-Teacher

Emptiness

Emptiness lives in a plain, bleak house with no furniture.
Her front lawn is dried up and is now just a patch of hard dirt.
She wears a gray heavy sweatshirt with a hood over her head,
and she wears plain black pants with big pockets.
The exterior of her house is a mess,
there are termites devouring the vine covered wood,
and there is rust and fungi everywhere.
She doesn't leave the house for unnecessary reasons,
only for groceries every two weeks so.
Her car is old and rusty and barely works.
Even her friends can't seem to fill that empty space inside her.
Shy tries to comfort her and sings softly to Emptiness.
Depression just sits with her and occasionally comments on some things.
Emptiness works from her office staring at the screen all day.
When she doesn't work, she just sits at the window staring
at the house across the street in envy at Happiness's house.

Mina Ghandi, 4th Grade
Strawberry Point School, Marin County
Lulu Monti, Classroom Teacher
Terri Glass, Poet-Teacher

Joy

Joy is the color green
like the beautiful trees.
Joy is a panda munching
on bamboo.
Joy is going to Hawaii
and going down a waterslide.
Joy is like cake
at midnight.
Joy is me and my baseball team
winning the World Series.
Joy is a whistle in the wind
making harmony.

Rory Dunlap, 5th Grade
Pleasant Valley Elementary, Marin County
Kathryn Hardy, Classroom Teacher
Lea Aschkenas, Poet-Teacher

Writing Ourselves/
Writing our Future

I Am From Black History

I am from Shea butter
From kanekalon and blue magic
I am from the smell of a hot comb heating up on the stove
Bumped ends and ruffled socks
It sounds like beads and barrettes dancing in my hair
I am from the sun flower,
cocoa butter being rubbed in my face
by elders on a Sunday morning
I am from line dancing and storytelling
from my grandma and her sisters and brothers
I am from warm hugs and Sunday dinners after a long day at church
From "Don't be coming in and out of my house"
And "No ripping and running"
I am from praying
Praying to God for my soul to keep
I am from the Motherland
Collard greens and cornbread
From blasting music on the Sabbath Day
To clean and prep talks from Nana before we go on a trip
I am from love, sympathy, warmth
I am from Black history.

Harmony Diggs, 12th Grade
Big Picture Ukiah at South Valley High School, Mendocino County
Kirsten Turner, Classroom Teacher
Bill Churchill, Poet-Teacher

carousel

I draft the words in my head
the way I did with this poem
    (i swear they were so much cleaner on paper),
rehearsing the lines over
    and over
memorizing them to the brink of insanity
    (i'm sane tho)
My thoughts go round
    and round
like they're tangled up in a merry-go-round spinning again
    and again
    (it's dizzying, my heart is no longer in sync with)
my body, it's shaking from the ups
    and downs
but i'm sure it's all just in my head
    (isn't it?)

Vee Lee, 11th Grade
Freestyle Academy of Communication Arts & Technology,
Santa Clara County
Jason Greco, Classroom Teacher
Christine Moore, Poet-Teacher

Secrets of the World

The trees told me that the past can survive.
The wind told me that we are strong.
The sun told me apples are burgundy and delicious.
The rain told me that storms make plant life better.
The world told me and the animals to not give up.

Jack Gorman, 1st Grade
Alexander Valley School, Sonoma County
Shannon Hausman, Classroom Teacher
Brennan DeFrisco, Poet-Teacher

Not My Problem

I believe that I can only speak
for myself. I believe that chaos is not my
problem. I believe that hunger and starvation
are not my problem.

I believe that only I know me,
not others. I believe that bullying is not
my problem. I believe that anger and rudeness are
not my problem.

I believe in plans changing.
I believe that difference is not my problem.
I believe that war is not my problem.

I believe that even if things
are not my problem I still can fight
for them.

Leah Frink, 5th Grade
Trinidad Elementary School, Humboldt County
Shazia Steward, Classroom Teacher
Dan Zev Levinson, Poet-Teacher

Poetry Is

Poetry is the chains
Being lifted off of your shoulders
The bird
Flying free over our world
Comes from anywhere
If you look
Poetry can find you
In the darkest trench
Or the brightest sky
Poetry looks
Like any writing
But
Tastes a little sweeter
Feels like the warm touch
Of a mothers song
Poetry is yours
Hold it

Tommy Schaufler, 7th Grade
St. Simon Parish School, Santa Clara County
Jen Tibbils, Classroom Teacher
Christine Moore, Poet-Teacher

Not From Here

I'm not from here,
way calmer than L.A.
From poorness,
having to live with lots of family.
No space.
I am from being overprotected.
From gunshots and fear
to moving and peace.

Angel Ramirez, 11th Grade
Big Picture Ukiah at South Valley High School, Mendocino County
Jason Gardner, Advisor
Bill Churchill, Poet-Teacher

Dead Ends

I've abused her over the years
bleach on bleach on dye on dye on bleach
a lashing whip, the kind where the bruises
stay forever and ever
under all the hurt she's suffered
roots remain strong and black
the ends have split,
the texture more
akin to plastic than anything, now
"she's sacred" I was told
"never cut her" I was begged and pleaded
bounching under my little skull
I was too naive to see why she begged this of me
so I cut her
I look around me now, though
the short copper curtains around my eyes
past the evil wall of ignorance and indifference
and understand why
Complete viscera, all my relations

I know where they'll send us
I also know they'll never have my hair.

Kimimila (Kat) Iron Bull Sanchez, 12th Grade
Delta High School, Santa Cruz County
Jamie Cutter, Classroom Teacher
Elbina Rafizadeh, Poet-Teacher

Food and Family

I am In-N-Out, the smell of fresh food getting cooked,
the first time I tried it with my family;
the burger and fries that make me feel united with my family.
I am the color blue because it reminds me of the Dodgers.
I hear music from the TV because I am watching the Dodgers play.
I can taste the snacks and the food because it reminds of the first time
my family made BBQ, and they also brought Wing Stop.
The flavor of the wings reminded me of the first bite I took,
when I first tried it.
The flavor was mild hot, and the bbq wings and fries tasted fresh.
The ranch makes the wings and fries taste much better.

Sophia Winchell, 7th Grade
San Fernando Middle School, Los Angeles County
David Malley, Classroom Teacher
Juan Cardenas, Poet-Teacher

Sopa de Gallina

I am a unique flavor in the afternoon sopa de gallina,
when we do this all the time;
El Panadero in the mornings.
I need to choose the chicken, and it takes me diez minutos
to catch it; la minuta después de escuela.
I am their voices singing. The music is unique; pasión, labios rojos,
si paredes hablara, y me llamaran.
I am black and grey;
the colors that I like the most with a meaning that represents me,
like calm and boring.

Maycon Rivas, 7th Grade,
San Fernando Middle School Los Angeles County
David Malley, Classroom Teacher
Juan Cardenas, Poet-Teacher

From Cities to Woods

I am from sweet and sour oranges
From Spalding basketballs and Toms of Maine Toothpaste
I am from the dark green house on a lopsided hill,
and the rotting deck overlooking the garden with the sea in the distance
I am from towering redwoods and the piney smell of burning wood
I'm from the fireworks that celebrate our independence at the pool,
and piercing ice blue eyes that characterize me
From Bryan Koon and Marina MacLeod
I'm from the bottomless dishes and screaming siblings
From "keep looking" and "try again"
I'm from no bible but kindness, and no God but love
I'm from the rolling hills of Scotland, and the lonely forests of Canada,
to the flamboyant lights of Orange County, and the gothic buildings
of North Carolina
From the salty steak and paprikaed potatoes
I am from the soups made from my garden
From the sweet and sour family that raised me.

Cosmos MacLeod, 6th Grade
Pacific Community Charter School, Mendocino County
Isabel Kuniholm, Classroom Teacher
Blake More, Poet-Teacher

From a Ranch in the Mountains

I am from a ranch in the mountains,
from carne asada and quads.
I am from where like was raw and real,
hay, farm animals, nature's sounds, song.
I am from crosses hung high and scattered tools,
my father's hands fixing daily rules.
I am from caring loving brown eyes,
from Tio Pedro and Tia Lulu.
I'm from the tio that kept us moving
and the tia that cared.
From "Ponle ganas!" and "Think before you act."
I'm from Christians, home of love and respect.
From Santa Rosa and Mexico,
tamales, meat, any form (I don't know.)
From the little brother that accidentally rolled down the river bank,
unharmed and laughing.
I am from a ranch in the mountains.

Jesus Loya, 11th Grade
Big Picture Ukiah at South Valley High School, Mendocino County
Jason Gardner, Advisor
Bill Churchill, Poet-Teacher

The Waves in Snow

I am from surfboards and snowboards
From sany-sandwiches and hot, hot, hot, hot cocoa
The low valleys,
The high mountains,
The cold winters,
And the hot summers
I am from the redwoods and pines
Prickly, yet soft trees
I'm from the happy surf days
And the cold snow days
From "Don't give up"
And "it's just a dislocated shoulder"
I'm going from sitting around to playing hardcore sports
From the amazing mom to the hard-working dad
I'm from the "we don't need a religion"
I am from Point Arena, CA
The land of everything
Scrambled eggs and roasted chicken
From my sad stories of curiosity
that actually killed my cat

Cian Fahey, 7th Grade
Pacific Community Charter School, Mendocino County
Isabel Kuniholm, Classroom Teacher
Blake More, Poet-Teacher

There's a Kind of Silence

There's a kind of silence where dew drops hang from the trees like silver bells and the only
sound is of chirping birds.

There's a kind of silence when you think you have been forgotten

There's a kind of silence when you are lost in a world of blurred reality too shocked to speak

There's that kind of silence when you know something has gone wrong, only you can't
grasp what it is

There's that kind of silence when you grasp what happened

There's a kind of silence when the silver bells melt off the trees to be replaced by orange as
bright as fire

There's a kind of silence only you can't enjoy it

Sylvester Hales, 7th Grade
Coastal Grove Charter School, Humboldt County
Jenny Rushby, Classroom Teacher
Julie Hochfeld, Poet-Teacher

I am Batman

I am Batman because I do more things at night.
I am Batman because I help my family.
I am Batman because I create things in the night.
I am Batman because I have a helper, like Robin.
I am Batman because I do not have too many friends.
I am Batman because I do not sleep at night.

Leonardo Lopez Martinez, 7th Grade
San Fernando Middle School, Los Angeles County
David Malley, Classroom Teacher
Juan Cardenas, Poet-Teacher

Quiet Dawn

I am me, although very bewildered, and very thick headed.
I still feel as though I am me. My thoughts continuously swirl,
clouding my mind with my perception of who I am.
I feel the sensation as if one were sinking into sand
whenever I lay on my bed, as soft as feathers.
Yet I can't grasp an image of myself actually sinking into sand,
as if it were like a hidden sea buried deep.
I see the appearance of light in the sky before sunrise,
as a quiet dawn creeps as quietly as ever.
The shadows of the trees shrinking as the sun awakes.
I hear the birds singing in the distance;
the wind blowing ever so gently on my face.
A feeling as if it were in a dream. A feeling of nostalgia.

Luis Peña, 7th Grade
San Fernando Middle School, Los Angeles County
David Malley, Classroom Teacher
Juan Cardenas, Poet-Teacher

My Life, Salvadoran Pupusas

Pupusas, pupusas — do they bring back memories!
For me, cada vez que las pruebo me traen sentimientos encontrados
and sometimes it makes me feel sad,
a veces me traen sentimientos tristes.
Pero other times they make me feel happy.
Pupusas are love.
Pupusas are my life.
Las pupusas are everything that is nice.
I would eat pupusas forever and never get tired.
Los feelings I feel when eating them are very great.
Recordando mi casa me recuerda
a las pupusas because I like the pupusas and my dad too likes the pupusas.
And every Saturday, we're eating, and I like this food because it reminds me of a place where todo es suave, rico y crujiente de textura.
Normalmente siempre estoy con mi papá desde que estoy pequeña,
y cuando era pequeña, mi papá me hacía pupusas para que ya no estuviera triste, y eso me hacía feliz, ya que mi comida favorita son las pupusas.
Una canción que me representa se llama Nunca es suficiente para mí, porque a mi papá le gusta mucho y siempre la escucha.
Un color que me representa es el verde porque me recuerda a una selva, un paisaje hermoso y un cálido atardecer,
y un lugar lleno de misterio, con muchos tipos de animales por conocer y muchas flores hermosas, con el sonido de los pájaros cantando mientras oscurece.

Mia Arrazate, 7th Grade
San Fernando Middle School, Los Angeles County
Mrs. Alvarez, Classroom Teacher,
Juan Cardenas, Poet-Teacher

No Place

My special place...
I don't think I have one...
I can try and think all I want
But one won't come to mind

I feel like everyone
has had at least,
once, a safe place
they've had,
but have lost it

I've lost mine and
have never been able to
find it again.

I pray I will
once again
maybe build it
and find it.

April Veloz, 11th Grade
Delta High School, Santa Cruz County
Jamie Cutter, Classroom Teacher
Elbina Rafizadeh, Poet-Teacher

Is it Me?

I used to feel big, powerful, and strong.
But now I feel small and hidden.

I used to think that all the pieces of the world would just fall into place.
Now I feel like a ship lost at sea, not knowing what to do.

I used to be able to climb to the top of the highest peak.
Now I shy away at its pinnacles.

I used to believe that I was big, a giant, and important.
Now I feel like I have shrunk, not standing as tall.

I remember when I could play on the swings without my brain
flooding with thoughts.
I used to be able to use a switch, put everything on hold.
Now I can't.
I can't just play pretend.
Can't let the world pass by.

I used to not care about what I wore, or what I said.
Now I stay quiet, afraid that if I make a bold move,
I'll end up alone.

I wish I could not care.
I wish I would go back to being that little girl.
But I do care.
This is me, and
I am ready.

Claudia Kenyon, 6th Grade
Mill Valley Middle School, Marin County
Brenda Poletti, Classroom Teacher
Claire Blotter, Poet-Teacher

Cliché

My name is like a cliché, it will get
old but not today or tomorrow,
but trust me, it will in the future
like a softball glove it will be broken
in. My name is from a family that
fought in boarding schools to get home.
My name is from Germany where my grampa Gary
came from. My name is from
my great-grandma who fished in the middle
of the night because of her rights
that got taken away. My name is from
my great-great-grampa Jimmy
who brought back the Yurok and Hupa
dances and by now you know my
name will stick to you forever.

Lillian Dempewolf, 5th Grade
Trinidad Elementary School, Humboldt County
Shazia Steward, Classroom Teacher
Dan Zev Levinson, Poet-Teacher

After

The night after noon
The drip drip drop from the roof
after the rain
The flash of lightning
after thunder
The laughter after
a joke in the night
The sadness after
destruction
I am after my mother and
father but before another

Demetri Gai, 6th Grade
Jacoby Creek Elementary School, Humboldt County
Holly Couling, Classroom Teacher
Dan Zev Levinson, Poet-Teacher

I am Happy

A happy person never gives up
Be happy and your life will be long
Create fun things like games so people can play
Do kind things so people like to play with you
Even to people that do not like to play with you
Find friends and life will be easier for you and you will
Get good grades your parents will be proud of you
Hanimi would even be proud of you
It takes a lot to impress Hanimi, he is very strong
Jets are fast, I think you knew that already, what
Kind of maniac would fight Hanimi
Lol they would lose to Hanimi
My best friend is Megami
No I know what you are thinking he crashes out
Oh then he summons him
Pat yourself on the back you are lucky he's not there
Quit thinking you can beat him
Rest it is night
Stop eating, it is time to move to our new home
Tap the door first to see
Up there, I am so happy it is a body guard
Vet I have a pet, it needs to go
Wow I did not know you had a cat
X-ray now
Yeet the cat out the window
Zap it now.

Bowie O'Dell, 3rd Grade
Manchester School, Mendocino County
Goija Post & Laura Gonzales, Classroom Teachers
Blake More, Poet-Teacher

Respect

I breathe in discrimination
I breathe out respect
no hesitation
Respect is a flower ready to bloom
in a dull room
Respect isn't earned
It's owned at birth
So, don't make someone hurt
On the inside I know I don't fit standards
On the outside I remember looking at my calendar
Imagine life's just a video game
which you're close to accomplishing
but hearing respect every day
makes me feel perfect every way
I don't fear discrimination
It fears me

Jose Vasquez Montero, 5th Grade
Roseland Elementary, Sonoma County
Denise Zaleski, Classroom Teacher
Lisa Shulman, Poet-Teacher

I Like You, But I Don't Like You

What I like about Legos
is you can be creative
What I don't like about creative
is that people copy everybody
What I like about everybody
is that we are all different
What I don't like about different
is that people judge you
What I like about you
is that you are amazing
What I don't like about amazing
is sometimes it is not big enough to describe something
What I like about something
is that it reminds me of my love for Legos.

Juanita Ramirez Alvarado, 5th Grade
Roseland Elementary, Sonoma County
Denise Zaleski, Classroom Teacher
Lisa Shulman, Poet-Teacher

Untitled

Completely extraordinary
More than I could write
dance and be unordinary
Be like no other
different from the others
Like a rhythm
a sound
Be like no other
Don't be the same
No lines between
a page
No colors
on a picture
No sound
to music
Be like no other

Aubrey Koifman, 5th Grade
Fair Oaks School, Los Angeles County
Ericka Irwin, Classroom Teacher
Alice Pero, Poet-Teacher

Unmatched Love

I don't compare myself to others
For I know my parents did their best,
They love me with all their hearts,
And gave me all they possessed.

Their sacrifices were immense,
Their struggles hard to bear,
They work tirelessly for me
To make sure I have a great life.

They may have not had much,
But what they shared,
Gave me all the love that they have
And showed me care.

So, I don't look at others,
And wonder why I'm not like them,
For my parents did their best,
And that's what matters.

I may not have all that I desire,
But I have their love and support,
And that's more than anything
For them I found my comfort.

So, I don't compare myself to others,
For I know my parents did their best,
and through love I've found my worth,
And in their eyes I'm truly blessed.

Arianna Alcala, 6th Grade
Roseland Elementary, Sonoma County
Madeline Salonga, Classroom Teacher
Lisa Shulman, Poet-Teacher

I Am

I am a shining gem,
I am a lion protecting my loved ones,
I am seaweed swaying in the ocean,
I am a shooting star bright in the night sky,
I am a patient clock taking my sweet time,
I am a strong soccer ball being kicked,
I am a tree standing tall in bad winds,
I am a bird soaring through the sky,
I am months slowly passing by,
I am a school learning new things
I Am Me.

Diana Jaramillo, 3rd Grade
Chenoweth Elementary School, Merced County
Amy Brown, Classroom Teacher
Dawn Trook, Poet-Teacher

Face Caterpillar

I am a man
I am brave and bold
I wonder if I will ever be young again
I hear too much
I see all the people mourning for their losses
I want inner somberness
I am a man
I pretend that I am fine but I am really not
I feel insane
I touch my lip and I feel my face caterpillar
I worry that I will never feel inner peace
I cry "why am I so different"
I understand that things change
but why so fast
I say may be alright
I dream that I can be younger
but I know that will never happen again
I try to feel better sometimes
I hope other people don't have to feel this
I am a new man

Max O. Post-Leib, 8th Grade
Manchester Elementary School, Mendocino County
Goija Post, Classroom Teacher
Blake More, Poet-Teacher

The Same
after Francisco Alarcón

We are all
the same

Like crayons
in a box

Like clouds
floating outside

Like words
on a paper

Like a group of birds
in the sky

Like noodles
in spaghetti

Like flags
of countries

Like a bunch of trees
in a forest

Like the regions
of California

Like soccer balls
on the field

Like leaves
on an oak tree

Like rocks
on the beach

Like letters
in the alphabet

Like stars
in the sky

Like sea creatures
in the ocean

Each of us
so different

Group Poem, 4th Grade
Tomales Elementary School, Marin County
Ben Demsher, Classroom Teacher
Virginia Barrett, Poet-Teacher

I'm Here to Change the World

My friends know me
as the girl who stands
in front of the crowd, speaking
my mind with ease, my heart
skipping a beat,
but still calm.

My neighbor knows me
as the girl who leaves
the paper at his door,
so he doesn't have to
go out in the cold.

My family knows me
as the girl who loves acting
and being in the spotlight,
thriving under pressure.

But people don't know
how someday I want
to change the world,
help people in their
times of need. I want
to be the voice for
the people who don't
have one.

Allison Sullivan, 5th Grade
Pleasant Valley Elementary, Marin County
Kathryn Hardy, Classroom Teacher
Lea Aschkenas, Poet-Teacher

This is Me

My grandparents know me
as the girl who walks on stage
and becomes a new person.

My closet knows me
as the one who can never
choose an outfit immediately.

My chickens know me
as the one who always
visits their nesting box
and chases them around
to pet their feathers.

But nobody knows that,
in my free time, I write down
story settings, characters,
and actions, the pen
touching the paper
with ink spilling out
of it, the characters
coming to life in my head.

Georgia McEachern, 5th Grade
Pleasant Valley Elementary, Marin County
Angela Villaluna, Classroom Teacher
Lea Aschkenas, Poet-Teacher

You Can be Anything

You can be artful.
You can be like my dad 20 years ago.
You can be a cloud floating in the sky.
You can be more relaxed than the dead.
You can choose to freeze a popsicle.
You can be a wise sage.
You can be a beautiful flower.
You can have as much incoming as you want.
But always remember, you always need at least one reason.

Conor DeVore, 3rd Grade
Edna Maguire Elementary School, Marin County
Teresa Shern, Classroom Teacher
Emilie Lygren, Poet-Teacher

I Am

I am a majestic elk slinking through the moonlight.
I am the voice of bliss inside you.
I am a brass trumpet, a staple of good luck.
I am a copper coin hiding in the wasteland.
"Comme, j'aime La Vie!" the voice I am
screams inside you.
I am the soul inside the survivors.
I am the melancholy storm awaiting you.
I am the one keeping you climbing the mountain
and when you get there
I'll be with you
planting the flag,
long live nature, as it brings us together as one.

Mac Flanigan, 4th Grade
Vieja Valley Elementary, Santa Barbara County
Tairy Birkley, Classroom Teacher
Cie Gumucio, Poet-Teacher

Me

I am the crash of ocean waves
I am the boom of drums
I am the melody of the bird
I am the tiger with fire in its blood
I am the moon bringing light to the darkness
I am the backbone that keeps all sturdy
I am the book that is filled with stories
I am the butterfly taking its first flight
Who but I could hold the world in their palm
so gently
so kindly
so wisely

Niya Frisella, 6th Grade
Mill Valley Middle School, Marin County
Bethany Bloomston, Classroom Teacher
Virginia Barrett, Poet-Teacher

My Writing

I write like a wave getting pulled back from the sand into the sea.
I write like a fox's paw steps, delicate and silent.
I write like an eel slipping back into its underwater cave.
I write like the clouds in the sky looking over the hills below.
I write like flames spreading through the trees.
I write like the smooth surface of a eucalyptus tree under its rough bark.
I write like a phoenix feather swaying in the gentle breeze.
I write like the stripes on a zebra's coat, each so pure and detailed.
I write like gravel on a path, digging deeper from the footsteps above.
I write like the red bellies of piranha scales running along the bottom.
I write like the movement of a river,
like a frog jumping from each lily pad to the next.
I write like a griffin's tail, following its wings up in the air.
I write like a bee's wings.
I write like the crackle of the fireplace, the storm,
the hurricane outside, outside of the rough and bumpy brick walls
surrounding me.
I write like a tree's fruit, each dropping on the shaded grass below.
I write like smoke rising from a chimney,
I write like me.

Alexandra Mohtashemi, 4th Grade
Montecito Union School, Santa Barbara County
Heather Bruski, Classroom Teacher
Cie Gumucio, Poet-Teacher

Middle Child

You are a streetlight
No one really notices you
You are always there
You give light to everyone around you
You make sure they feel safe
in dark times but in your dark
times no one notices you
You're the one brightening the road
You make sure everyone is safe
You aren't afraid to say things
for how it is and it doesn't matter
if it's good or bad
You will always expose the truth
at the road
Everyone needs someone like you
You are a streetlight

Jacqueline Zamora Rodriguez, 6th Grade
Roseland Elementary, Sonoma County
Jacqueline Lopez, Classroom Teacher
Lisa Shulman, Poet-Teacher

The Raging Sea

I imagine a ship on
raging seas as the moon
shined brightly in the dark
just listen to the wind,
the future is upon
us all

Siddhartha Arturo Sil, 1st Grade
Edna Maguire Elementary School, Marin County
Shana Stewart, Classroom Teacher
Emilie Lygren, Poet-Teacher

I Come From
(Paiute, a Native American Tribe)

I come like a brave warrior
fighting for their water.

I come from a land of
the great Sierra Nevadas.

I come from towering rocks
acting as a backbone for my tribe.

I come from a land
dry and hot during the day,
but when dusk comes,
it's cold and crisp.

I am made of seeds and berries.

I am made of fierce eyes
that make up all the battles
my ancestors have fought for me.

Morgan Wilder, 7th Grade
Mountain School, Del Norte County
Julie Shunk, Classroom Teacher
Terri Glass, Poet-Teacher

Imaginations

The Foxes

The Lightning Fox
    Taught me
        How to throw lightning bolts
            In the rain

The Firefox
    Taught the furriest falcon
        How to throw fireballs
            In the sun

The Foxes
    Have secrets to tell you:
        They can fly to the moon

In the forest of myself, I feel the tickle
I hear a scratch
I see a lightning fox
    I become lightning
I see a Firefox
    I become fire
If I were lightning, I would have speed
    I would have so, so much speed
If I were the fire
    I have power, and I DO have power

                      I am fast and powerful!

                Nathan Castillo Vail, 3rd Grade
            Coleman Elementary School, Marin County
              Kimberly Goodhope, Classroom Teacher
                      Lulu Wong, Poet-Teacher

Parrot

I see giant tentacles
in the distance.
I hear booms from cannons.
I feel the leathery coat
of Captain Jack.
I taste fish
from my last meal.
I smell salt water
from waves crashing
against the ship.
I flap my way up to the crows' nest
as a tentacle smashes
against the ship.
I wish I could be a real pirate
like the others.

Desmond Hanley, 4th Grade
Pleasant Valley Elementary, Marin County
Jenna Maioriello, Classroom Teacher
Lea Aschkenas, Poet-Teacher

Under the Banyan Sky

Under the Banyan Sky is a slanted lagoon,
Where ocean waves crash on the rough sand.
The water is turquoise, the clouds float above,
And gentle waves roll over the rocks below.

Under the Banyan Sky is a shore,
Where the sun shines all day.
My feet get wet, my hair gets messy,
And my skin turns golden from the sun.

The Banyan Sky holds memories—

Chasing geckos after eating açaí bowls,
And laughing while the breeze blows.
I remember the sand sticking to me,
Knots in my hair,
And my eyes red from the sea.

Under the Banyan Sky, the days feel long,
And the nights go fast.
Lanikai Beach, two mountains stand tall,
And in the hills, walruses nap together,

Soaking up the summer sun.

Under the Banyan Sky, the sea is deep and blue.
It holds animals from long ago,
And colorful fish hiding in coral and seaweed.
Masters of camouflage.

Under the Banyan Sky is a hotel,
Ko'Olina, right by the sea.
It's the picture in a frame
The salty breeze and soft waves feel like a lullaby.

It's where time slows down,
And everything feels calm and happy.

Yael Shenassafar, 7th Grade
Pilgrim School, Los Angeles County
Dominic Rossi, Classroom Teacher
Carlos Ornelas, Poet-Teacher

The Door to My Imagination

Through my bedroom door
gray fur, sharp eyes into a brightly lit world
by a single tap of a finger.
Only I can open it; wind rustling, leaves dropping to the ground
you stomp through the autumn leaves with a crunch.
You walk into a grand oak tree,
on the other side is water so clear and shiny
that you could drink it.
You dive to the bottom all sound goes
You are in peace.
You see a small boat not far from you
you go to the surface and see the pale midnight sky
the stars are so bright you reach for them
you climb to the moon and
see there a constellation that is your door
you slowly open it with a creak
running to tell about your adventures
but it's empty you look into the pantry
and go back to the moon and there is a pencil
you grab it putting your fingers slowly around it
drawing that plastic star on your bedroom ceiling
and go to sleep next to 1,000 wolves.

Lala Mendez, 4th Grade
Vieja Valley Elementary, Santa Barbara County
Montse Vega, Classroom Teacher
Cie Gumucio, Poet-Teacher

Fractured Star

how swirled must a mind be

        grinding inadequacy looking inside
        his light is

    Cracked.

  he turns away, to the star people
Shouts his own fears, dressed up
    as words of wary

they land and echo and etch, in others
       but spill over the lines, the star
  people see the drips and scream
  Bursting heads, muddled
  with Plague

he offers silver
  Cages and Chains
    like the broken stars before him

and the fallen stars

          and stolen stars

      Disappear

Athena Driesen, 11th Grade
Freestyle Academy of Communication Arts & Technology,
Santa Clara County
Jason Greco, Classroom Teacher
Christine Moore, Poet-Teacher

Recipe for Neon Rainbow Stars

First, pour in 3 tablespoons of moon dust.
Next, add some moon ocean water.
After, use 6 of the rainbow's colors.
Add a pinch of glitter.
Mix inside a seashell.
Melt some moonlight.
Add some lightning, too!
Especially add some black holes for an extra shine!
Twinkle on some stardust.
Sunlight will do the trick to add some extra magical touch!
Add some mermaid tears.
Add some pearls for a shine.
And especially add some gold.
Whisk in two unicorn horns.
Add some jellyfish tentacles.

Genesis Sanchez, 4th Grade
Hope Elementary School, Santa Barbara County
Isao Sugano, Classroom Teacher
Cie Gumucio, Poet-Teacher

Take Me Down to Earth

Take me down, take me
down to Earth.

Where the waves crash
by and the new flowers birth.

Take me down, take me
down to Earth.

For too long I've waited,
for too long I've searched.

Take me down, take me
down to Earth.

Way up high, I drift through
the sky, see all futures through my eyes
though I wish to be a
normal humankind.

Take me down, take me
down to Earth.

So, now I rest among
the stars, alone in space
so long and far of where
I truly long to be.

Take me down, take me
down to Earth.

*This poem is about
a child who lives in space
and has all the most
powerful abilities but
wants to be normal.*

Cynthia Marsolan, 5th Grade
Freshwater Elementary School, Humboldt County
Dara Soto, Classroom Teacher
Dan Zev Levinson, Poet-Teacher

Something Strange

I am the fast black panther
                                and for some reason, I have antlers.
                                     Now I jump to the beach.
At the beach

                                           I see a banner.
               On the banner, it said to spend the night at the beach.
                         So, I spend the night at the beach.

                              I have to sleep in a hamper.
                        After my horrible night of sleep,
                             I became a tap dancer.
                                No one knows that
                              I am a famous dancer.
I am full of anger
               that NO ONE knows how good of a dancer I am.

Iris Riley, 3rd Grade
Coleman Elementary School, Marin County
Kimberly Goodhope, Classroom Teacher
Lulu Wong, Poet-Teacher

The Unsung Hero

I live my days hidden from the world,
cold, stale, musty air fills my lungs,
intoxicated by the smell of lost hope, hostility, helplessness, and sadness.
Day by day, I am used for my strength, and my durability, nothing else.
I know nothing other than these dark tunnels that slice away every hope
I have found peace within myself,
like a tear carving a path down my dreary muzzle.
I heard a myth from a wise old friend that the sun is alive,
where the luminescent gold light trickles
through your fur and into your soul.
Like a stream full of life and ever abundant hope
I asked my wise old friend if he has acquired such feeling before,
he said the day he came to this earth, he felt it.
It soothed him, cared for him,
like a mother lulling her child into a peaceful state.
I crave the sun day by day, even though I have never been touched
by the light of day. I long for this the way the desert must crave the
rain, but somehow lives without it.
But I go day by day hauling ore and rock through the demoralizing
mines to find no treasure at the end.
I feel the way the wind feels as it erodes mountains, shapes dunes,
and spreads seeds without recognition.
Maybe one day I'll hear the songbirds,
feel the gold light on my fur,
smell the warm air,
and taste the rich grass that absorbs all that I long for
down here, in the mines.

Izzy Wells, 11th Grade
Sierra Academy of Expeditionary Learning, Nevada County
Marika Beck, Classroom Teachers
Kirsten Casey, Poet-Teacher

How I Would Paint

How I would paint my mind
A long vast page of a book
A jar of apple cider bobbing on the water's surface
Ripped pieces of paper
A sea glass blue, so fine it can disappear
The winter trees covered in thick, soft snow
The gravity of a black hole
Turning me into a kite

How I would paint patience
An empty waiting room
A frog waiting for a fly to come by
A monarch in Mexico waiting for summer
The purple plumage of a bird
A Mockingjay waiting for a song to sing
A minute passing

How I would paint blood
A knife stabbing
A crimson so red it burns
The wax of a candle that flickered on November second
A twilight red slowly disappearing in the sky
the first drop of red coming from a wound

How I would paint falling
The crumbling side of a rock cliff
Land so far you would think it's from another world
Wind coming so fast at you, for some reason your floating
A fragile being floating to the bone crushing ground
Black like your closed eyes

How I would paint secrets
A corked green bottle
A whispering mouth
The oceans depth
A dark blue smeared on someone's mouth covering it
White cloth so fine it will never hold someone else's whispers
A broken wall, rubble and bricks scattered
A far gone friendship

													Noora Sulem, 5th Grade
													Strawberry Point School, Marin County
													Daniel Gasparini, Classroom Teacher
													Terri Glass, Poet-Teacher

Untitled

Unthinkable.
That'd be us, stretched out against your velveteen couch
The sand dunes of your back storming as the trickles of my
showerhead puddle in your pores
Your throat bobbing.
Us on the sprinkler golf course, your thighs are the columns to
my colosseum
In what other transient stretch of time but this balmy July
could I love you?
But against *Les Halles* and your missus,
Under Poland's skylines, swimming in the dark
You know how to do it right--
With the stallions in the barracks and the studs in the bar
To a destructible end
Here, we don't have to hide
As businessmen on the New York metro
Or in a kleptomaniac's hotel room or from
The Scotch-reeking hands of that father of yours
We can drive that tractor and smash its windows
Lay across the bumper, dribble ginger-ale
Through this skin-peeling sunburn
The convenience store's aloe vera, that where your lips lie
For the caveman times knew us better than
My mother to whom my letters will never deliver
My DNA is in your throat, so what if your wife knows?
But you'd rather the river rush up your lungs than be seen with me
So what if they know?

Lisa Zheng
Youth Poet Laureate, Sonoma County

Woman in the Water

(Ekphrastic poem to a painting called *Dive In* by Susan McKay)

Midafternoon on the riverside,
she jumps in with a splash.
The dark blue of her swimsuit
contrasting deeply with the bright green
rocks underneath her.
Her hands pull back
allowing her to glide underneath the water,
allowing her to fly past the bright orange fish
striking against the light teal water above.
She breathes out, exhaling gently
preparing to surface. After breathing,
she will dive back down
for her fingers have yet to caress
the softness hidden deep
in the water below.

Evelyn Allen, 5th Grade
Mountain School, Del Norte County
Julie Shunk, Classroom Teacher
Terri Glass, Poet-Teacher

Maybe it Was

Maybe the artist wanted you to be found
Maybe he didn't want you to make a sound

Maybe he wanted the waves to crash as loud as thunder
Maybe he wanted you to just stand there and wonder

No bright colors maybe you were bland
Or maybe you were waiting for somebody to hold your hand
Maybe you just like standing in the sand

Maybe you could feel winter's salty blow
Maybe you could taste it in the air

Maybe you couldn't reach the icy sea
Maybe you could, just you didn't want to freeze your tea

Maybe the sky wasn't dark
Maybe it was you
Maybe your heart was dark and cold like the sea

Maybe the sky wasn't the sky and the ocean wasn't the ocean
The landscape was you
You made it cold
You made it salty
You made it dark

Maybe you were staring out at the sea
But maybe you were staring right at me

Amelie Lamy, 7th Grade
St. Simon Parish School, Santa Clara County
Jen Tibbils, Classroom Teacher
Christine Moore, Poet-Teacher

Animal Alliteration

Floppy fish flopping in the water.
Silly snakes singing sad songs.
Fat fish thinking while playing the fiddle.
Precious pink pigs painting pink pictures.
Purple pandas popping popcorn.
Hungry hippopotamus hitting hard.
Leaping lumping lions laughing.
Jolly jaguars jumping jump rope.
Giant giraffes eating great grapes.
Frightened frogs freaking out.
Lazy lamas licking large lollipops.
Outstanding octopuses eating avocados under the bridge.
Diving dog digging in the water for a dinosaur.
Patient Pegasus walking over the pretty earth.
Zippy zebras zigzagging around the zoo.
Feisty fox finding fudge-flammable frogs.
Beautiful bunnies bobbing back to bags of bananas.
Elegant elephants eating everything.
Coyotes cascading over crates.
Tigers trying out tricycles under trees.
Illuminated iguana illuminating the imagination.
Poetry panda writing a poem.

Group Poem, 3rd Grade
San Ramon Elementary School, Marin County
Rachel Ojeda, Jen Cabaud, Fiona Gilmartin, Classroom Teachers
Virginia Barrett, Poet-Teacher

Poetry

[Found Word Poem]

The elated iguana devoured
poems with the aardvark.
The books were as plump
as pomegranates and huckleberries.
Their faces were illumined
with the scrumptious treats.
Some of the books lay akimbo
on the magnificent shelves.
Sitting on the beach, watching
the undulating ocean, strumming
their ukuleles in their sanctum,
little did they know serendipity
had planned a spectacular
journey for them.

Group Poem, 6th Grade
Mill Valley Middle School, Marin County
Bethany Bloomston, Classroom Teacher
Virginia Barrett, Poet-Teacher

The Door to My Imagination

The door to my imagination isn't just a regular door. It's made of tears. Tears that I have cried. If you try to open it when you are agitated it will stay locked. My imagination is calm and quiet. It won't let you disturb the peace. When you unlock the door to my imagination, you will find yourself on a stage, a crowd in front of you, waiting to see what will happen. You start to sing. It comes out like a rough ocean, than it gets softer as you start to sway with the music... but you trip and fall, and when you get up, there's no more stage, no more crowd. It's just a pitch-black room with a door. A different door. One made from the scales of an aqua blue, green, and purple dragon. You reach to try and touch the door, but as you do, you stumble onto a beach. You dive under the waves with a splash! When you look back at your legs, they're not legs anymore, but instead a ruby red tail. You spot a pod of dolphins and swim to them. As they jump, you jump with them. Fish of every color swirl around you. As you surface to the top of the water to take a breath, you see a tsunami towering above you. You swim toward it and try to get enough speed to go through it. The tsunami is just too powerful. It pulls you under the water. A blur of blue is all you see. You look around for safety, heart thumping. You spot a cave and swim to it before the next wave hits. You reach the cave in time, just before the wall of water descends upon you. In the cave you find you're in a hollow volcano. On the other side of the volcano there is another door. This one is made of lava. You are scared to touch it, but you find the courage to do so. As you reach for the door handle, you seem to pull water with you, accidentally splashing the door. The door turns to rock. But as you look closely at the door, you notice a handprint. It fits your hand perfectly. A golden spiral flashes around your hand. The stone door breaks. You peer inside the next room and hear a droplet of water hit a puddle. One foot after the other, you step inside the room and see a pond surrounded by crystal clear waterfalls. You take of your shoes off and dip your feet in. The water seems to be calling to you so you step further in. You can't resist anymore, so you dive under. Water floods your ears. In a flash, you are back to the first door. You reach for the handle but let go and walk away, already knowing what you will find in my imagination.

Olivia DeMarco, 4th Grade
Montecito Union School, Santa Barbara County
Shannon Gallup, Classroom Teacher
Cie Gumucio, Poet-Teacher

The Natural World

Sunset

The sunset comes
from the ripe nectarine
falling from the tree
into a river
of blue water
It becomes night
with the fish swimming
as the stars in the sky
as the fish get caught
Stars fade away
Sunrise is a child
grabbing the nectarine
from the water
He takes it home
and sunrise and sunset are gone

Romy Amash, 6th Grade
Fair Oaks School, Los Angeles County
Ericka Irwin, Classroom Teacher
Alice Pero, Poet-Teacher

What the Rain Told Me

after Mary Oliver's *Last Night the Rain Spoke to Me*

Last night the rain told me
if you don't give me joy then
I will start making thunderstorms
I promise that I will give you joy
Please tell me if this good
Today is a good day the trees are bright
and ready for the spring also the flowers
It just rained hard
but it was okay because there was a rainbow that smelled like flowers
and also fresh
grass
It sounded like a Bang!! on the metal
Afterwards the rain said I won't rain no more because that was the best joy
EVER!!!

Brodey Saeteurn, 3rd Grade
Chenoweth Elementary School, Merced County
Meuy Saeteurn, Classroom Teacher
Dawn Trook, Poet-Teacher

Our Beautiful Mother Earth

We treat the Earth badly even though she is good to us.
We betray her with global warming,
making the Antarctica warm and glaciers melt.

Mother Nature helps flowers bloom in a troubled world.
She makes it rain, so her grass can turn bright green.
We have feelings, and so does Mother Earth.

When we throw trash on the street it makes Mother Earth cry.
I feel devastated when I see videos of polar bears struggling to
find safety while their home disappears.

Sometimes I think to myself how horrible people are to treat
Mother Earth so badly, after all the beauty and love she gives us.

Kayla Hernandez, 7th Grade
Nicasio School, Marin County
Kristy Snaith, Classroom Teacher
Michele Rivers, Poet-Teacher

Our Amazing Oceans

Our oceans are deep, dark, mysterious places, filled with
mystical creatures from starfish to dolphins to whales.
On our shores, small sneaky crabs skedaddle along the hot sand.

Above, a flock of seagulls fly, diving into the rough
ocean in search of fish.
Waves crash on the gritty golden shore.
The salty air is thick with moisture.

I wonder what is below the deep dark oceans.
Stingrays glide like they are flying, while sea turtles
stay on the surface and bathe in the sunshine on beaches.
It's crazy to think that we have explored so little of these amazing waters.
Imagine what else lies beneath yet to be discovered.

Lya Uzri, 7th Grade
Nicasio School, Marin County
Kristy Snaith, Classroom Teacher
Michele Rivers, Poet-Teacher

My Special Place

The beach is a special place
so cozy and beautiful
peaceful and amazing
I can hear the seagulls and birds singing
it is music to my ears
with the blankets it's so cozy
I find beautiful shells
with the water so perfect
I get snacks and food
The people are so happy and calm
I look at the awesome and beautiful clouds and sky
I can see the buildings
And the dogs playing
And there I was at the beautiful beach
such a special place

Myles Pirtle, 3rd Grade
Chenoweth Elementary School, Merced County
Meuy Saeteurn, Classroom Teacher
Dawn Trook, Poet-Teacher

Our Oceans

Our oceans are full of mysteries like a good book.
They are filled with fish that swim together.
Their majestic waves bounce off the rocks like fountains.

All the fish swim in harmony like an orchestra in tune,
My heart is like the sea with so many colors shining brightly.
The ocean is full of water swelling and churning like the struggles in life.

The sea wraps around me like my mother's arms.
The rippling waves are like an argument.
It seems like a privilege to be able to watch them.

Ben Kozubik, 4th Grade
Nicasio School, Marin County
Megan Young, Classroom Teacher
Michele Rivers, Poet-Teacher

Elephants and Mice How Nice

Awake with eyes wide and open—
there's an elephant in the room.
You go upstairs and find an elephant in the kitchen,
everywhere you go, there's an elephant.
And then that's when you find out people are mice
running to school for dear life- everybody is mice!
And there is an elephant in the room,
big and gray and you look small and gray.
Surely everybody is doomed.

Avery Chun, 5th Grade
Strawberry Point School, Marin County
Rachel Quek, Classroom Teacher
Terri Glass, Poet-Teacher

Three Haiku

See grass walk away
Small, green, soft, bent, dull, standing
A happy Haiku

I feel trees moving
Smelling moist air covering
Confused, happy, Haiku

Rapidly angry
Clouds are ancient
They rotate by

Ava McCloud, 5th Grade
Kashia Elementary School, Sonoma County
Michele Taylor-Jones, Classroom Teacher
Brian R. Martens, Poet-Teacher

If You Were a Butterfly Like Me

Seeing bright skies with fluffy clouds
Feeling the soft touch of a velvet rose
Tasting the sweet nectar of a poppy
Hearing the rustling of leaves on a tree
Smelling the salty sea as you pass over
That's what you would know if you were a
butterfly
like me

Ellie Marsh, 3rd Grade
Montecito Union School, Santa Barbara County
Kathy Trent, Classroom Teacher
Kimbrough Ernest, Poet-Teacher

Eagles Wolves Winter Stars and Rain They're All Related

The feather of an eagle tickles my nose
The shadow of a wolf scars me
Winter is upon us

Glittering snow almost as pretty as you
The bright stars shine above the moon
The flame of the rain is over by dusk

Found poem inspired by N. Scott Momaday

Cressida Maccubbin, 3rd Grade
Montecito Union School, Santa Barbara County
Lisa Monson, Classroom Teacher
Kimbrough Ernest, Poet-Teacher

Mother Earth's Feelings

I love Mother Earth
When she is scared
I hear her crying for help
When she is happy
Her land is green
When I pick up trash
She is less scared

Every time it rains
It is Mother Earth tearing up
Every time the wind blows
It is Mother Earth calling for help
I am grateful to her
I love how she provides for us

Anthony Barajas, 4th Grade
Nicasio School, Marin County
Megan Young, Classroom Teacher
Michele Rivers, Poet-Teacher

The Movingness

The movingness was perfectly still,
unexpecting
It ran away into the blue light
It swam through the soft waves
as it shone with starry clouds
shaped as the sun
They moved towards the wind
coming from
a different direction
They sang and laughed
They got moved by force
from absolutely nothing

Liv Sarkovich, 6th Grade
Fair Oaks School, Los Angeles County
Ericka Irwin, Classroom Teacher
Alice Pero, Poet-Teacher

King of the Woods Beyond

Owls hoot
piercing the darkness
lighting a
torch in the
shadow
like a soft wind in the
cattails
a beak curved like a branch laden with
fruit
the coat of
golden feathers
in your fog covered
home
not seen by passerby
your nest is a work of art
the inside soft as
cotton
you are the
emperor
of birds
powerful
a panther
of the forest
silent
on wings
that stretch to the
sky
clever
like a quick, sneaky
fox
the mice bow
down to you

begging for
peace
but you win
oh king of birds
you are strong as the
mountains deep
leader of the
woods beyond

Milena Barker, 4th Grade
Park Elementary School, Marin County
Leslie Bernstein, Classroom Teacher
Claire Blotter, Poet-Teacher

Mother of the Sea

My feet stand on the harsh cliffside, my eyes search for the sight of
A thirty-five-ton mammal, breeching into flight
The harsh wind is at my back when I see a tale
There's an excited, screaming voice in my heart when I spot the whale
Rough, ragged rocks tumble down, down, down
If I were to jump, I would certainly drown
I look out to the sea reflecting the sky
Knowing there's a whole world below the surface, calling "don't be shy!"

My feet dig into the shore, thousands of grains milled by time
The picture-book landscape just fits like a rhyme
Dark ominous clouds gather overhead
The torrential downpour will stir the seabed
The sea foam crashes against the shore
The rain goes from sprinkle, to drizzle, to pour
The white waves pummel the beaches-soaked sands
The foam glides nearer, to where I stand
My legs bring me forward, the current pulls me down
I take a deep breath, while my toes leave the ground

My feet float in the foreign high seas
No pressure of gravity, they're finally freed
This wild, wild deep, part of no known nation
This is truly a marvel of Mother Nature's creation
This is a place where the squalls reach a peak
And those who seem mighty, suddenly turn weak

Problems fade away, and life seems unreal
Krill pass by, then a turtle, and a seal
A shoal of herring form a tightly knit bunch
While sharks below are planning their lunch
Sea stars cling onto shells for their lives
While oysters hide precious pearls deep inside
Immeasurable distances away, in the depths of the sea
Nightmarish creatures exist, only seen in my dreams

I hear a sound, that instills great fear
But it's mere beauty, draws me near
Through the water, I see the silhouette
Of a ginormous great creature, enjoying the sunset
Watching everyone in the seas, making certain all is well
She feels the ocean and every part of the swell
From the galaxies in her eyes to her white patterned tail
She is the most majestic being, this humpback whale
This is the realization, that for the fate of our future
We must do all we can to make sure we don't lose her

Anna Neto, 6th Grade
Nicasio School, Marin County
Kristy Snaith, Classroom Teacher
Michele Rivers, Poet-Teacher

I Wish to Grow Like the Sea Wind

I wish to ride the sea in
search of nothing but
the cold wind gashing my face
with the sounds of waves slamming
in repeat until it becomes
a part of me.
I wish to get lost in deep
thought of everything I'm concerned
about to learn and grow from
the cautions.

Axel Tripp, 8th Grade
Orleans Elementary School, Humboldt County
Clarissa Readen, Luke Parkhurst, and Andie Butler-Crosby,
Classroom Teachers
Dan Zev Levinson, Poet-Teacher

Grass

What language do you speak?
I speak of ants and wind and branches swaying.
What is your job?
My job is to cushion your feet, to rustle in the evening breeze.
Doesn't it hurt when people step upon you, and pluck you from the soil beneath you?
No. It feels like life, and also death. But I feel no pain.
What do you hear upon your field?
I hear laughter, joy, and sadness upon my field.
What do you see upon your field?
I see war and peace, cold winters, and hot summers.
I see crows plucking worms from the ground.
What do you feel upon your field?
I feel the warm sun seeping into my soul, the feet brushing my soil.
I feel groundhogs making their homes in the dirt, and squirrels burying their acorns.
With whom do you share blood?
I share blood with none, but the mother earth and her children.
Are you one blade of grass or all of them?
I am one of many. I am the speaker of those who grew from the ground.
What's your name?
Grass.

Ella Cha, 4th Grade
St. Simon Parish School, Santa Clara County
Stephanie Shatto, Classroom Teacher
Christine Moore, Poet-Teacher

My Thoughts on Our Oceans

Our Oceans
Immensely divine like bowls of sapphires shimmering in the sunlight
Our seven seas perfectly breathtaking like the seven petals of the Budda's lotus flower
The Atlantic, a massive body of saline paradise for muscular sharks and tiny seahorses alike
Her angry, yet beautiful waves reach high, only to fail to grab what they are grasping for
The Atlantic Ocean, ours to cherish and protect
But nevertheless, we do not

Our oceans so tremendously deep and dark
Seas as vast as the celestial sky
The Pacific wears a bold ring of hot, angry, ruby red volcanoes
She is home to sea-otters, quiet sea turtles and elegant manta rays
Their habitat once a safe and soothing place
Now there isn't a fluid ounce of ocean that doesn't contain pollution

Our seas once so pristine, now made impure by mankind's arrogance
Everyday islands of trash gather and rise like a Hawaiian Volcano
Every minute, innocent sea creatures perish from shameful toxins
Soon enough it could be too late to turn the tides

Standing on the shore watching pieces of plastic float by
I start to wonder what we can do to fix this destruction
How could we have damaged so many beautiful homes
I really hope our future is brighter than our present

Daniella Maloney Flores, 8th Grade
Nicasio School, Marin County
Kristy Snaith, Classroom Teacher
Michele Rivers, Poet-Teacher

Chime of the Wind

Oh the chime of the wind,
the melody of the breeze,
the splash of the river,
the force of trees,
the blaze of thunder,
the frost of ice,
the inferno of fire,
the gust of the ocean,
the fangs of the canyon.
Life itself we all are home.

Micah Dunn, 4th Grade
Arcata Elementary School, Humboldt County
Katie Piner, Classroom Teacher
Dan Zev Levinson, Poet-Teacher

AXOLOTL

An amazing site to see when swimming
eXtraordinary powers that might takes hours
Oh No! only a few hundred left
Lucky you are to see one, they love their freedom
Only if you love them, you will like them
Till you see one, you probably won't believe they exist
Little they are, but so powerful.

Siena Filian, 3rd Grade
Vallecito Elementary, Marin County
Ann Weiss, Classroom Teacher
Terri Glass, Poet-Teacher

Three Haiku

Baby bird chirping
Mama went to find the worms
Chirp, chirp breakfast time.

The grass is a plant
Hay and trees are plants also
Sunny days are nice.

The birds are chirping
I saw squirrels climbing a tree
It was a redwood tree.

Ayden Marrufo-McCloud, 5th Grade
Kashia Elementary School, Sonoma County
Michele Taylor-Jones, Classroom Teacher
Brian R. Martens, Poet-Teacher

The Hand of Nature

This hand brought you the scent
of flowers after a big storm.
This hand is keeping you alive.
This hand waters your plants.
This hand sacrifices everything for you.
And yet after all it has done
we still treat it poorly.
This hand is dying soon.
We will have no hand soon.
Our planet will be artificial.
Soon our life will crumble
into a million pieces. Soon
there will be no scent,
no more life, no more water,
     nothing.

Charlotte Shaw, 5th Grade
Garfield Elementary School, Humboldt County
Alaina Kelley, Classroom Teacher
Dan Zev Levinson, Poet-Teacher

Hawk　　vs.　　Snake

hawk glides up in   snake slithers to fear
pride, silent and bold
                            hoping to be spared
hawk looking, flying, spying   snake still
                            cowering, hiding
hawk high and royal   in dread
with wing of flame   snake low and
                            lame, a leaf
                            among many others

        together better
        apart an enemy

Manuel Vielma, 5th Grade
Skyfish School, Humboldt County
Blair Soffe, Classroom Teacher
Dan Zev Levinson, Poet-Teacher

Dazzling Snakes

A snake is like a fish
swimming silently
through a stream
like a breeze
in the middle of
a warm summer night,
scales dazzling in
the grey moonlight
like diamonds
in the rough,
its muscles moving
day and night
like a shark
swimming while
it sleeps.
Snakes.

Carter Crosswell, 4th Grade
Park Elementary School, Marin County
Leslie Bernstein, Classroom Teacher
Claire Blotter, Poet-Teacher

Where We're at Now

The Growing Name

I wore a name that wasn't mine
It fit, but not quite right
I smiled the way they taught me to
And kept my edges tight

The mirror holds a stranger's gaze
So close, and yet not clear.
I chase the voice I hear inside
But doubt is always near.

The world still wants a shape to hold
A box to press me through
Though I mourn who I have lost
I'm reaching for what's true.

Jeriko Fleming, 11th Grade
Willits High School, Mendocino County
Katrina Hall, Classroom Teacher
Bill Churchill, Poet-Teacher

Three Haiku

Hear trees in the wind
Talking to me now, happy
Surprise leaves falling

Deer playing in woods
Talking to trees listening
Happy, joyful, kind

Missing native women
Killed, missing, murdered, unknown
Nobody did crap

Jeremiah Patrick, 5th Grade
Kashia Elementary School, Sonoma County
Michele Taylor-Jones, Classroom Teacher
Brian R. Martens, Poet-Teacher

Erase My Birthright

your heavy palms crushed our people in their creases
ignored the decades of suffering,
scrubbed them clean and folded them up,
you put them in your pocket
where they remained untouched
we are in your hands, but our history is not yours.

you scraped us into beings our ancestors would
not recognize as their own
ripped our language out of our souls
burned the yearning of its characters onto our tongues
beat our bones out of our bodies with each forbidden utterance,
ashes fall from our lips with every banned syllable

our vernacular was everything that tethered us together
the fibers that intertwined to unite hearts,
the thread that pierced the individual pieces and made them whole,
our soda bread and butter
you have reduced our words to cinders

all we wanted was the freedom to declare that our homeland was ours,
but liberation came with arms
we were labeled terrorists for daring to love our country,
despairingly dreaming of the day it would be unified under our people
conflict on innocent neighborhood roads marred the lands we tended to
bombs rattled sparrows from their perches

peace was no solace for the mourning

the sky became as dark as the fingerprints that stained our flag,
blood mottled fabric, stitched together by stories and truths
a symbol of the liberty we desired
a remembrance of our hope that was shot and buried
we had to die so our republic could live

we do not learn from your books
we do not claim the narrative you wrote for us
our history is burned into our blood

you have erased our birthright
robbed us of the recognition of generations of trauma,
we are ripped apart and left to the wind

this is what history will remember most cruelly.

Juno Phipps, 11th Grade
Marin School of the Arts at Novato High School, Marin County
Rebeca Pollack, Classroom Teacher
Maxine Flasher-Düzgüneş, Poet-Teacher

Where the Moon Meets the Sun, the Sun Meets the Moon

I used to think I had time
I used to think I had enough days to capture key moments in life
I used to think a lot about life

Now I think about the end

Time falls between my fingers and I let it f
                                              a
                                            L
                                                L

The dreams I once held firmly   s.. l.. i... p...

I no longer crave to wonder about tomorrow
I no longer crave to speak

My mind grows b l a n k

Sudden noises shake me wake

It's been 22 hours since I have been able to properly sleep

When I close my eyes I enter a world of darkness
My dreams are filled with rage
My heart in distress
Windows, doors, blinds, and weapons scare me
I'm on high alert with nowhere to run

I won't allow the darkness to swallow me whole
So I watch it
Sacrificing my sleep to feel peace
I watch the moon meet the sun and the sun meet the moon
Forms of light that never miss

Tears that sparkle against the moon drip down my face
I melt in exhaustion; soon we'll wake up
Where the moon meets the sun, the sun **will** meet the moon

Jasmine Guerrero Sevilla
Youth Poet Laureate, Santa Barbara County

Skin

Am I my skin?
My body
nothing more
My soul overlooked

Skin
Judged before being seen
Judged before being known
Flesh
Sticking to my bones like a bad rash.

Mark after mark
scar after scar
Stretching, shrinking, stretching
Never consistent
Never "true to size"

Skin
Everyone has it
different shapes, different sizes
Why am I so quickly judged
When I was born the way I was?

Inescapable
Trapped in the body I have
Trapped in the surroundings of meat and fat
Trapped with my eyes
my ears
my mouth
and nose

So once more I ask,
Am I my skin?

                                      Athena Marino DeFrates, 10th Grade
                                      Willits High School, Mendocino County
                                              Katrina Hall, Classroom Teacher
                                                  Bill Churchill, Poet-Teacher

Untitled

Some things that fire can destroy are homes, trees, buildings, and nature.
Some things fire can't destroy are hope, love, courage, and dreams.
The fire looked like it was smokey and big, and could
destroy anything in its way.
The fire smelled like burning wood , which made it smell smokey.
I felt scared when I saw the fire because I had never seen a fire that close.
My family told me to look outside and see; and deep inside I still felt safe
that the fire wasn't affecting my family or my house.
The fire burned homes, but it couldn't take away my hope.
Flames rose up, but my dream of helping nature still stood.
Smoke filled the sky, but my heart held on to believing in everybody.
Even if everything turns to ash,
I still believe in kindness because nothing can take away kindness.
I carry this dream like a flame in my chest, to help people
because many people got hurt because of the fire.

Aurora Rocha, 5th Grade
Morningside Elementary School, Los Angeles County
Mrs. Ramos, Classroom Teacher
Jessica M. Wilson, Poet-Teacher

Brasil!

I hear the "screech" of the rainbow macaws
flying in the bright blue sky.
I hear the "sizzle" of the rice and beans in a pot.
I hear the "zzzz" of the mosquitoes.
I hear the "creak" of the crickets in the night.
I hear salesmen screaming, "Churros!"

                                                              Lucy DeLaney, 4th Grade
                                Pleasant Valley Elementary, Marin County
                                        Sandy O'Brien, Classroom Teacher
                                            Lea Aschkenas, Poet-Teacher

Please Don't Leave

You say you never will,
You say I need to breathe

But how can I breathe
When you yell at me?
Knocking the wind out of me
I fall on my back every time

I want to trust you,
I really do
But how do I know what you're saying is true?

I fear I've grown attached
Like a band-aid stuck too long
So please
Be kind to my heart
I'm afraid that if you leave,
I might fall apart

You treat me so bad,
You treat me so well,
Do you really love me?
Sometimes, it's hard to tell

Salisa Leon, 11th Grade
Willits High School, Mendocino County
Katrina Hall, Classroom Teacher
Bill Churchill, Poet-Teacher

Listen

Listen to that drop of rain,
crowded thoughts, crowded brains,
intricate designs,
complicated minds,
some a dull line,
some a sharp shine.

Scarlett Fierro, 5th Grade
Freshwater Elementary School, Humboldt County
Dara Soto, Classroom Teacher
Dan Zev Levinson, Poet-Teacher

The Fires

The fire burned the Rabbit Museum, but it couldn't burn my faith in God.
When I saw the fire, I was surprised by how fast it was spreading.
I felt bad about the people and their houses.
Though deep inside, I still believe in God, and I know he will protect me and my family.
Flames rose up, but my faith in God still stood.

Esteban Solis, 5th Grade
Morningside Elementary School, Los Angeles County
Mrs. Ramos, Classroom Teacher
Jessica M. Wilson, Poet-Teacher

Big Orange Flame

Fire burns and burns but it can't destroy my faith.
The big orange flame gets bigger and bigger each day,
the smell gets stronger and stronger each day that passes.
I felt terrible when I saw the fire take down houses, one by one.
Flames rose up, but my love still stood.
Smoke filled the sky, but my heart held on to my loved ones.
I carry on to my dream; to save people's lives and become a doctor.

Jackson Gomez, 5th Grade
Morningside Elementary School, Los Angeles County
Mrs. Ramos, Classroom Teacher
Jessica M. Wilson, Poet-Teacher

In What Language Should I Speak to You?

I. Bird
In a feathery whisper?
Peering into the depths
of the nests
of your eyes?
Or should I call
for you
from the sky above,
yearning to show you
the winds game of Twister.
Should I rise
until I softly disappear
and join the sound
of beaks and bodies?
Or should I fall,
bathe in your words?
Will above call me?
I think the sky
has always been
this way.

II. Fire
Maybe I should drift
into your ears
and slip
my lost prayer for peace
between your lips,
char the rough
ends of your hair?
Should I humm to you
in shoes of smoke

as rubies dance
from your eyes?
Salt from your brow
and blistering on your skin,
a flakey ashen jacket
you may never shed.
You keep your distance
beyond the frame of light.
Will you step forward
and should I spit sparks?
If I do,
you will fall
to your knees in pain,
a burning palazzo.
Should I wait for August
or should I speak now?

   III. Summer
I know,
I will run to you barefoot,
wriggling my toes
into the cool dirt.
Offer you all I have,
a ripe peach,
a hair tie,
an eyelash.
Should I brush topaz
on your fingers or
a string of beads
for your ankle?
I will wait

in this liminal space,
floating between realities.

Meet me in our tent, in
the depths of the tides,
behind the mosaic.

Tess Belger, 12th Grade
Tamalpais High School, Marin County
Barbara Ditz, Classroom Teacher
Maxine Flasher-Düzgüneş, Poet-Teacher

just friends

Confusion
Never have I felt this way about someone before
Especially not a girl
Not when I'm a girl

We were just friends
Sharing a moment of laughter and joy
What changed?
Why do I look at her differently now?
Why does my heart race when her smiling face pops up in my brain?
Why do my palms get sweaty and my mind goes crazy and don't know what to say and…

We were just friends
I finally had a bestie in my grade
Haven't had that since I was 9
My older friends are nice
But she's nicer

But we were just friends
With our inside jokes
And secret signs
We only met this year
So when did it change?

We were just friends!
But now every time we're together it's awkward and I don't understand why
I don't understand the feelings I feel about her
I don't understand how I thought I was normal but now look at me
I don't understand who to blame
Is it me?

We were just friends

I don't understand why all of a sudden I have a crush on my friend
Because we were just friends!
Nothing special
But now I can't stop thinking
About her
About me

About us

She doesn't like me back
I know that for a fact
So why am I jealous?
Why am I angry?
Why do I feel hurt, sad, and lost
All about a friend

Because we *are* just friends...

Right?

Madeline Meyers, 7th Grade
Pilgrim School, Los Angeles County
Dominic Rossi, Classroom Teacher
Carlos Ornelas, Poet-Teacher

None of us are Natives

We all had to come there, somehow
to the land of the free
following the soft glow
of the moon staring at us
hoping we make it safe.

The language of the world
drifting together into one,
with dreams of dancing
through neighborhoods of
copy and paste houses.

Here in the land of opportunity
with infinite chances to be
who you want to be
like the galaxies of stars
we share overhead.

The land of the free
the land of hope
the land of the people
who were here first
and the ones who came later.

Olivia Smith, 11th Grade
Delta Charter High School, Santa Cruz County
Jamie Cutter, Classroom Teacher
Elbina Rafizadeh, Poet-Teacher

Smack!

Smack!

The baseball hit me
in the head, riding my bike
to the baseball field.
Two toddlers watched
from a big redwood.

I was going as fast
as a sea urchin in a pool. Before I crashed
all I saw was the laces of the ball
closing in on my head.
I crashed; all happened at once.
Toddlers jumped from the tree,
ran to me and kicked me.

Viktor Azbill, 8th Grade
Kashia Elementary School, Sonoma County
Michele Taylor-Jones, Classroom Teacher
Brian R. Martens, Poet-Teacher

A Girl's Only Option

Tucked in the corner of a wooden drawer
She waits for a shoulder to sit on
A head to hug,
Hair to hide,
And for hands strong enough to lift her

An intricate scarf,
Whose beauty breathes through embroidered beads
Intricately sewn on like whispered dreams

As she carries the burden bled into a little girls mind,
Once hidden beneath veils of abuse and tradition,
She steps out only to go back in,
Her country saw her as a lone piece of clothing,
While women saw her sewn into their identities.
A hijab,
A girl's only option.
To be shot if not covered up.

The lone silence of a woman's voice
A noise,
-normal like an ambulance.
A replacement for their freedom.

Trembling,
Choking,
دار نگه محکم
زنجیر نه هستند سرپناه ها حجاب از برخی.»
"Hold fast.
Some veils are shelter, not chains,"
they told her while gasping for air.

But Satisfaction finally struck when she revealed her lips,
Unveiled her hair
And let go as time stopped.

                                                      Sayeh Shenassafar, 7th Grade
                                              Pilgrim School, Los Angeles County
                                                Dominic Rossi, Classroom Teacher
                                                    Carlos Ornelas, Poet-Teacher

How Am I Supposed to Cry

How am I supposed to cry?
I've spent too many years
My tears stained into my pillowcase
My sheet draped over the bed I rot in

So how am I supposed to
When I have no tears left?
Mom yelling at me makes the tears start to flood
Or thinking about the past, and being scared about the future
I think about Dad and what he's said

I was like the rain
It would never stop
But now I don't

Now don't get me wrong, I'm not happy
Just cried so much there are no tears left

But one time I did
I thought it was impossible

There was a girl so special
I loved her beyond the moon
To Jupiter and the distant sun
To the next galaxy, as far as possible
Together, we spent every minute
I needed every second

Until one day she called
Said: sorry, but I want to break up.
Her voice flatlining

I tried to cough something up but nothing would flow
So I hung up the phone and said I have to go
It was then a tear fell

I felt it on my right cheek first

Like water in a desert
Like winter's first rain

It was then I knew
A drop could conspire
In these eyes of mine
Filled with nothing but you

> **Timothy Gene Southwick,** 10th Grade
> Willits High School, Mendocino County
> Katrina Hall, Classroom Teacher
> Bill Churchill, Poet-Teacher

One Sweet Dream

I was in the grass just
laying there watching the stars.
Blankets on me with a pillow,
with popcorn, and drinks.
The birds are humming in my ear. Seeing
the moon, imagining astronauts
on the moon. Seeing butterflies flying in the sky.
All the trees are shaking around
because it's so windy.
Seeing Spider Man swinging his webs all around
to save the day. Seeing Stephen Curry
shooting hoops, making every shot like it's nothing.
Seeing Kobe Bryant hitting jump shots super
easy. Seeing Messi scoring goals all day.
Justin Jefferson catching every ball that goes to him.
Seeing me being a future NBA player.

Kaedyn Comer, 3rd Grade
Chenoweth Elementary School, Merced County
Meuy Saeteurn, Classroom Teacher
Dawn Trook, Poet-Teacher

Three Haiku

Call of Duty dead
I explode like hurricane
Mad, mad, mad, mad, mad.

Another year gone
Travelers shades all colors
straw sandals on foot.

Refreshing and cool
Love is a sweet summer rain
That washes the world.

Linkn Carver, 8th Grade
Kashia Elementary School, Sonoma County
Michele Taylor-Jones, Classroom Teacher
Brian R. Martens, Poet-Teacher

It Would Be Easier if We Were Less Frail

You set the cabin air to circulate
as the dusky blackness
grips the car

again comes the roiling in the distance,
summer blending campfire and the Camp Fire.
Fire a rhythm and ritual,
common as kid fingers smeared with huckleberry.

You learn to negotiate altitude:
Hold your head above smoke
breathe in hitches

When flames roll in at home,
they remind you of summers outside,
till rugs must be rolled beneath doors

>	Blocking
>	civilization's evidence

>	Blocking
>	the Nixle alerts,

>	Blocking
>	the unending panic,

>	Blocking

unable to block frailty

If flames came, we would char and fall away
there is nothing in us that would go on
there is nothing in us beyond sinew,

nothing essential.
Nothing given to lift up our unclean heads
from the water,
or taken to guarantee our standing
different to the tide;

It would be easier if we were less frail.

Frej Barty
Mendocino County Youth Poet Laureate

Enjoy It

When I was one, I relied on my mom to live.
When I was two, I ran around my house
screaming and not getting in trouble.
When I was three everyone adored me and thought I was so cute.
When I was four, I would dance in the rain and do whatever I wanted,
not caring what people thought of me.
When I was five, I would sing, laugh and dance with my friends,
and no one hated me.
When I was six, I would eat all the candy that I wanted not caring
about the way I looked.
When I was eight, I had a lot of friends, but some people were mean.
When I was nine, I started brushing my hair and taking time to get
ready in the morning.
When I was ten, I cared what people thought about me,
not everyone was my friend even if I was nice.
When I was eleven, everything I did mattered,
how I looked, who my friends were.
I didn't like that.
Now I am twelve,
I know what people think about me.
Some people aren't my friends and aren't nice.
I miss the days when I didn't care what people thought about me,
but I do care.
No matter how hard I try not to,
I will always care.
Enjoy the days when you can run and scream and dance and sing.
Enjoy the days when you're young.

Ava Desmond, 6th Grade
Mill Valley Middle School, Marin County
Brenda Poletti, Classroom Teacher
Claire Blotter, Poet-Teacher

Letters, Gifts & Odes

Ode to Life

The first time I opened to the world
I cried and laughed
The second time I opened to the world
I was new and different
The third time I opened to the world
I was interested and confused
The fourth time I opened to the world
I was cranky and didn't understand
The last time I opened to the world
I was loved and cared for and that's how it was

Ginger DeWoody, 3rd Grade
Montecito Union School, Santa Barbara County
Kathy Trent, Classroom Teacher
Kimbrough Ernest, Poet-Teacher

I Am Giving You...

I'll give you this song that came from a bird,
so you can sing sadness away.
I'll give you a pile of autumn leaves to jump in.

I'll give you the scent of crisp winter air.
I'll give you a beautiful waterfall so you can remember
what it was like to let your imagination run free.

I'll give you the soft touch of a fluffy blanket so you can snuggle up
and watch a movie.
I'll give you the taste of delicious food to make your taste buds happy.
I'll give you laughter to make all your days happy.

I'll give you the love you feel for a dog.
I'll give you photos to look at and remember everything.

I'll give you a telescope to look up and see the stars.
I'll give you the sky to hear the breeze.

I'll give you joyness and sadness,
so you can have everything.

Malin Kunes, 4th Grade
Mountain View Elementary, Santa Barbara County
Katherine James, Classroom Teacher
Cie Gumucio, Poet-Teacher

Ode to Taylor Swift

Oh Taylor! Oh Taylor!
Your song makes me rise.
Oh Ms. Swift! Oh Ms. Swift!
I shall hold on to your lullabies.

Your golden blond hair,
your sparkly blue eyes—
Oh Taylor! Oh Taylor!
Just you make me rise.

I listen to your melodies every single day.
They make me lift to the sky.
Your first album of butterflies and country—
the great beat makes me fly!

Then your next golden piece
rare as the princess in a tower.
The beat makes me infinite,
yet as gentle as a flower.

Your 3rd is a plumish vibe
filled with fairy tales.
When I listen to your beat
it succeeds all my fails.

Your 4th as red as roses,
a true fun friend beat.
Its mixture and variety
lifts me off my feet.

Your 5th the beach.
Your 6th the shadow.
Your 7th the pink sunset.
Your 8th the fog.

Your 9th the wood.
Your 10th the night.
Your 11th tells us you're
not done typewriting yet.

You're generous and caring.
You're creative and smart.
I wish to meet you soon.
You have a shining heart.

Tatum Goldberg, 3rd Grade
Montecito Union School, Santa Barbara County
Lisa Monson, Classroom Teacher
Kimbrough Ernest, Poet-Teacher

A Letter from the Moon

Dear miners,
for months now
as I wax and wane in the liquid night
you file down
into tunneling holes in the earth
the walls jagged and dark
like the scars of a burnt hillside, blackened and stripped of its soul
I see you return, dusty and tired,
with the scent of mildew and candle wick
pressed into your leather jackets
like the damp air that hangs in the attic after a storm
I rise above the ponderosa pines,
piles of their needles clumped at the trunks
like a flock of ducklings surrounding their mother
that sit clustered around the manicured lawns like
cloaked statues
the garden's foliage, glistens in my light
like emerald glass tucked into a towering mosaic of stars
I see the pounds of harvested rubble and earth
scattered with fluorite, quartz, pyrite and granite
that you work so tirelessly for
as you dig deeper, and deeper
towards the swirling molten core of earth
that shrieks at every blow like a ringing in my ears
black powder and dynamite dust lingering
in every breath you take
I have longed to ask you why
why you hide your face from the warmth of the sun, the comfort
of day, what could be worth
the sacrifice?

-with love, Moon

Amara Berry, 11th Grade
Sierra Academy of Expeditionary Learning, Nevada County
Marika Beck, Classroom Teacher
Kirsten Casey, Poet-Teacher

Dear Lovely Sky,

As I flew through your shifting branches of starlight last night,
I became lost in your splendor
The scent of linseed thick on the breeze, like walnuts and soil
Whirling, spinning, twisting, cartwheeling, falling
Wings thrown back in ecstasy at the spiraling aurora of you

I had only intended to stay in the sky wandering
For an hour or so, nothing more
The taste of oil paint and straw on my tongue, like an echo of home
You were unusually bright that night, dazzling as oil streetlights on evening dew
when I glanced up at you, I was enchanted.

And I fell away from the world

I implore you for forgiveness,
I beg of you, do not think less of me for wandering
I am but a humble bird, it is in my nature to fly
When I tore my gaze away from you at last, the earth was green, Saint Remy was awakening.
The caress of the breeze singing in my ears, gentle as a downy nest
When I descended again at last, the sun was smiling at me from where she rose,
Laughing at my foolishness!

"Look at this bird who has fallen for the sky!
She does not see the worst of it,
The tempests and the showers, like a crying child
The vengeful winds and the merciless gales, like the bitter sting of limes
This fool has fallen for but a moment in time!"

If I could only feel the stars under my wings again, like fish swimming through the sky
If I could see the twisting patterns of the heavens under your eye again

You are the most luminous thing I have ever laid my eyes upon.
Whorls of starlight stretching into infinity,
I fear if I fly at night again I shall never touch down.

Yours in admiration from afar,
A bird

Callie Marsh, 11th Grade
Sierra Academy of Expeditionary Learning, Nevada County
Marika Beck, Classroom Teacher
Kirsten Casey, Poet-Teacher

Dear Poem

Dear poem, I'm sorry that I
don't want to write you, yet I
have to do this assignment
but I have no spark to my inspiration.
I'm so sorry that I won't fill up the
page, having no choice but to
surrender to the clinging arms
of boredom. I wish to go to
sleep, being I have nothing
to do. OOPS . . . I guess I'm not sorry,
poem, so I guess this poem
was an accident.

Sequoia Dervin, 6th Grade
Whitethorn Elementary School, Humboldt
Mr. D, Classroom Teacher
Dan Zev Levinson, Poet-Teacher

Dear Vincent,

For so long,
I have waited
Longing to be seen
For the life I carry
Through my swirling,
Frigid winds

You see the world
The way a delicate hummingbird
Sees a simple petunia

As an explosion
Of vibrant ultramarine blue

Your weary eyes
Guide your trembling hands
Each brush stroke
Swift and bold
Like a gentle gust of wind
Swaying against the lonely Cypress

Oh, Vincent
The unburdened minds
Shame you
Dismiss me, your unstable sky
As you manifest
The stars that fill me
Their constellations
A map across my infinite cobalt shawl
draped loosely around my neck
Only we, the misunderstood
Can understand

Love,
The Sky

Natalie Robins, 11th Grade
Sierra Academy of Expeditionary Learning, Nevada County
Marika Beck, Classroom Teacher
Kirsten Casey, Poet-Teacher

Dear Stars and Skies,

I want to tell you about the rainforest.
Here, a speckled yellow feline glides silently
through the droopy, high leaves.
Here, there are skies as pink as flamingos,
filled with birds that look as though they were molded
from a rainbow after a hurricane.
A secret cave lies deep in the heart of the trees
past the snakes scattered in olive scales.
The big opening is stuffed with mysteries
like the lost whisper of a sleeping tiger.
Small black-winged creatures wake as the sun falls
like a feather dropped off a macaw,
the star-scattered sky wakes and the curiosities
of the night get to work.
Chirps of a cricket rise and fall like a sweet melody,
along with the growls and soft sways
as if they are in a band.
Once the vines stop dancing and the sun wakes up to a
peachy-red sky,
if anything in this world is more beautiful
than the blue-feathered birds and brown beige rodents
skittering through the logs, I don't know it yet.

From, Valerie to the infinite skies above

Valerie Zell, 5th Grade
Mountain View Elementary, Santa Barbara County
Nate Latta, Classroom Teacher
Cie Gumucio, Poet-Teacher

Dear Father Patrick,

Before I wake each morning, I remember why I am here.
I remember the soft smiles, and the laughs like morning birdsong.
I remember your church, painted white like soft clouds.
And I remember what you told me once:
You said that God is above us, and the devil is below.
I write to you because I understand now.
And because I wonder —
Might this pickaxe carve straight to hell?

For these white Sierra mountains border my horizons.
Their peaks remind me of elegant towers,
their slopes, ivory ramparts.
Their forests of Eden wake me with the songs of mockingbirds,
And their rivers flow like liquid quartz.
I have to wonder — Is this the heaven you dreamed about?

If it is, then that must mean that below my feet is fire and brimstone.
That if I dug a hole as deep as these mountains are tall,
I would surely burst straight into hell.
Yet that is precisely why I am here,
flocking along with all the others like ants to honey.
We dig desperately in the dark, deeper.
Always, ceaselessly, deeper.
We follow the gold, laid out like breadcrumbs,
As it winds ever farther from the paradise above.
The canaries scream at us that this is wrong,
And the rats gnaw at our boots, trying to warn us off.
But always we are told: "More! Dig farther!"
And so we do.

My skin and lungs are despoiled by the earth's black blood.
My candle struggles mightily to hold back its darkness now,
As the cold crawls like a sickness into my bones.

The clamorous rattling and screeching of gears

Sounds to me like demons laughing in joy.

Sundays — I understand why they are called that now.
They are the only days that the sun shines on my back.
The only days I get to talk to God, and feel him above me.

I fear that all other days have been given to the devil.

Sincerely,
A humble miner

Jadon Castle-Haley, 11th Grade
Sierra Academy of Expeditionary Learning, Nevada County
Marika Beck, Classroom Teacher
Kirsten Casey, Poet-Teacher

An Ode to the Small Things

This is an ode to the small things.
The small things like the
pencil I am using right now.

Oh, the smelly things.
Mom's casserole.
My socks.

Oh, the pieces of bigger things.
The computer chip in the mother board.
The scientist, working on a
cure for an illness.

Oh, the mundane things.
Doing dishes,
sweeping and mopping,
school.

It all must be done in
order for everything to
work. Thank you small
things, for *everything*.

Fintan O'Dwyer, 6th Grade
Blue Lake Elementary School, Humboldt County
Michelle Gibbons, Molly Crandell, Stewart Millar,
Classroom Teachers
Dan Zev Levinson, Poet-Teacher

Dear Mom . . .

   I'm sorry for
eating the chocolate
   chips from on top
of the refrigerator
   that you were saving
for the cookies you
   were about to make
They were just so
   tempting and they
were my favorite kind
   You were at the
store to grab one
   last ingredient
Dad was outside and
   Jax, well I had
to give him some
   too so he wouldn't
tell, so technically I
   didn't eat all
of them, so please
   forgive me I just
couldn't help myself

      ~ *Parker*

Parker Budesa, 5th Grade
Coastal Grove Charter School, Humboldt County
Marjorie Bertsch, Classroom Teacher
Julie Hochfeld, Poet-Teacher

Ode to Cold Things

Glory be to cold things
to the snowboarding days in Mammoth
and the frigid mornings in Carp
to the crashing and bashing waves

Glory be to rock-solid icebergs
and the wet, soft, squishy noses
of Seamus and Taylor

Glory be to the huge night sky ahead
to all the things I have never explored

Avalon Carrington, 3rd Grade
Montecito Union School, Santa Barbara County
Jacki Hammer, Classroom Teacher
Kimbrough Ernest, Poet-Teacher

Ode to Black

Oh, how we love the color black.
It is the color of a Sharpie and a panther.
It smells like coal.
It tastes like tar and blackberries.
It sounds like paving a road.
It feels like an eraser.
Oh, how we love the color black.

Group Poem, 3rd Grade
Venetia Valley School, Marin County
Matthew Pope, Classroom Teacher
Virginia Barrett, Poet-Teacher

Ode to Blue

Blue is the sea with fish in the stars
taking the form of constellations
in the starry sky.
You have octopuses like the krakens
making peace and
the mighty protector of the sea,
your turquoise pet, the Leviathan
that has giant shiny blue scales
that make you proud.
Blue, you are the sky
with clouds
and stars.

Zack Mitchell, 4th Grade
Loma Verde School, Marin County
Cheriann Reed, Classroom Teacher
Claire Blotter, Poet-Teacher

Midnight Black

Oh, Black, you are burnt toast
like midnight black.
You're tar on the road,
a room with no lights on,
a desk with black papers scattered,
a black raven chasing a black mouse,
my shadow in bright sun light,
dead plants like a rotten banana,
a tinted window in a rocket ship,
the lead that fell out of a black
colored pencil,
shoes with black socks,
black stripes
on a flag.

Dylan Burke, 4th Grade
Park Elementary School, Marin County
Leslie Bernstein, Classroom Teacher
Claire Blotter, Poet-Teacher

Ode to Blue

You are the teal flower
Blooming in the wind.
You are the waves
In the ocean.
Oh blue
You are the paper
that is being drawn on.
You are the sweet blueberries
In my fridge.
You have a big heart
Like Uranus.
You are the bluejay
In the woods.
Oh blue
You are the pretty
Sapphire diamond.
Oh blue, Oh blue.

William Jimenez, 6th Grade
Roseland Elementary, Sonoma County
Madeline Salonga, Classroom Teacher
Lisa Shulman, Poet-Teacher

Green and Brown, the Perfect Pair

Green and brown, oh,
  green and brown
    you are the
      perfect pair
        you are
          the center
            of the forest
              giving breath to
              all the red
                berries and glowing
              blue rivers
Oh, Lady Green,
  you are as bright and
    majestic as a
      sparkling emerald hidden
        by the wisest
          willows tickling the
        surface of the river
And, Sir Brown,
  you are the warm
    cottage of hope in
      the deep dark
        forest the Black
          Forest of Germany
you are as gold
  as chamomile and
    honey tea
you are the pair of the fairy-
    tale woodland

Green, you are as cheerful
   as a clover freshly born in spring
     yet as calming as
       sweet fennel tea
Oh, you are the perfect pair!

Emilia Rauschecker, 4th Grade
Park Elementary School, Marin County
Leslie Bernstein, Classroom Teacher
Claire Blotter, Poet-Teacher

Cobalt

Cobalt is the
Ocean, sparkling
in the moonlight.
Cobalt is a
crayon, flowing with
imagination.
Cobalt is tears,
when bullies strike.
Cobalt is
calm, cool, and
collected.
Or
Cobalt is the wrath
of a dragon.
Cobalt is my color.

Charles Sullivan, 3rd Grade
Chenoweth Elementary School, Merced County
Amy Brown, Classroom Teacher
Dawn Trook, Poet-Teacher

Whale & Butterfly

Oh, Butterfly, you are so colorful high up in the sky.
My ocean family is jealous of how you fly.
I am a Whale, as old as the sun.
I've seen you fly freely but if you come into the ocean's waves,
there will be magic you have never seen.
There are fish of every color,
playing music inside the sea.
Octopi blend in so no one can see them.
If only you knew me, we would play
in the shipwrecks finding treasure.
We would ride on turtles.

If only you knew me.

Oh, Whale, your ocean home is very colorful,
cold as can be.
But, if you flew with me, we would see mountain
after mountain
with goats in bushes and tree after tree.
We would hear dogs barking,
and see cats climbing.
We would smell luscious hotdogs.
We would see kids on swings.

If only you knew me.

Lexi Lawton, 3rd Grade
Mountain View Elementary, Santa Barbara County
Holly Bosse, Karen McEachen, Classroom Teachers
Cie Gumucio, Poet-Teacher

Poet-Teacher Poems

Let Them Write

When all else fails... Let them write.
Give them the gift of poetry.
I don't mean assigned reading
I don't mean analyzing the rhymes written in dusty books,
I mean... give them the kindling to ignite the fire that already crackles
within their own voices.
Even the smallest sparks can be fanned to burn bright.

Give them an antidote to cure the ache inside their chests.
Maya Angelou once said, "There is no greater pain
than carrying an untold story inside of you."
So I say...

Let them write.

Let them tell the story burning inside of them
The one nobody else has ever asked to hear

Let them bend the rules and break the rhyme scheme
As long as they do it with intention.
Sometimes the only way to tell the truth is to bend it into something
that feels a little more
approachable.
A little more comfortable.
A little less vulnerable.
Because it's still their truth,
but a version of it that will land better on listening ears.

Most of my students tell me they don't like writing poetry.
They don't like navigating the maze that is metaphor -
They ask, "Why can't I just SAY WHAT I MEAN?! Literally!
Why do I have to describe my bedroom curtains being blue to
represent my endless flow of sad
tears when it's easier to say that I'm just sad?

Better yet - why do I even have to write about being sad in the first place!?"

I tell them they don't
I tell them to write about;
Memories,
puppies,
kitties,
sports,
Their heroes,
Their wishes,
food,
celebrities,
dinosaurs,
Donuts,
Their music,
Their dreams...

Whatever they want!
I try to let them write.

But they just stare back at me — puzzled.

I explain that Poems aren't puzzles,
Poems are mirrors—
Poems are windows—
Poems allow us look into the lives of people who are endlessly different than us
while at the same time letting us see ourselves reflected between their lines.
Fragments of identity refracting like sun off of every simile.

Poems are fists—
When you feel too scared to fight,
too weak to make change,
When your body can't go on...
Add more kindling.

Because your voice always can.
Poetry has that power.
Storytelling has that power.
Writing has that power.

So let them write.

If for nothing else...
let them write because when the keys of the keyboard click-clack
or the pencil on the paper skrit-stcraches
Poetry can be the much needed pause in a world that won't stop talking.
A quiet corner among the chaos.

A moment of silence for all the creative writing ideas that ended up scraped.
Tossed by a custodian into the trash.

And a moment of silence for all the kids that have ever felt the same way.

Poetry is a space in time where kids who don't always "fit in" get to exist fully -
Get to create a world for themselves.

I know not every student speaks sports.
I never did.
Some of you are like me -
Some of you speak stanzas.
Speak sparks.

So let them write.

Because while history might explain the past,

Poetry can help us to not repeat it.

While science might cure bodies,

Poetry cures hearts and minds.

And while math might build bridges,
Poetry reminds us why we choose to cross them time and time again.

So I say... Let. Them. Write

Dominic Rossi
Classroom Teacher, Pilgrim School
Los Angeles County

Big Girl Panties

This morning, I woke up with a mental swirling ah-ha moment,
I was afraid.
Afraid of what? I thought, as I reached for my dog and stroked
her soft, golden fur. She always comforts me, with her silent
adoration.
I pushed on with the question . . . What am I afraid of?
A simple question with a simple answer . . .
Not being good enough.

I'm a published writer,
For heaven's sake, my first book sold twenty-five thousand copies.
Isn't that proof?
Don't I qualify?
Nope!
The fearful terrors continue.
On a regular basis, I doubt myself as a writer,
It's crazy, I feel like a total fraud when saying "I'm a writer."

However, four hours later, I put on my big girl panties and did it!
Yep, I emailed my latest book to three friends—all fine writers—for
their review.
I then asked myself the question – what else am I afraid of?
Another answer instantly came - every type of rejection.

I thought about all the young poets I teach.
I tell them about being brave and sharing their poems with their
classmates.
To help students at recitals, I ask parents to raise their hands if they
are afraid of public speaking.
I imagine the kids might feel reassured when they see dozens of hands
raised to the ceiling.

Next week, when I start a new poetry program with about seventy-five fourth graders,
I'm going to share this breakthrough with them, and how I realized that I must resist being
trapped by what other people think of me.

I'll read them this poem.

Michele Rivers
Poet-Teacher, Marin County

Ars Poetica—Bolinas

The days are suddenly shorter; the scent of
brisk air when I wake, inviting melancholy

tied to winter need. Instinct buried deep,
that sunshine and sustenance will soon grow

scarce? But there's comforting memory as
well: heat from the fireplace blaze, a wet but

soothing thaw after sledding outside for hours.
Childhood leaves its imprints, remote and often

faded, only to swell at incongruous moments
like now, here in the late afternoon warmth, as

hundreds of seagulls circle above this lagoon,
white specks in the distance shimmering with

light against the western face of Tamalpais,
from the Miwok *támal pájis*, "coast mountain,"

an approximate translation they say. I was once
a mountain girl, but not this kind; no ocean

near, frozen ground for months, and snow swirling
as white shapes in wind *like these gulls* I could

write, if I wanted simile today but I don't. I just
want these gulls as gulls, rising and circling,

circling and soaring, and I want the pull of
the tide in and then out . . . waves of ache tangled

with rapture; this poem a rough decoding of
the fugitive sway.

Virginia Barrett
Poet-Teacher, Marin County
*"Ars Poetica—Bolinas" first appeared in
Burningword Literary Journal, April 2025*

Jostling with Gentrification

Gentrification, a double-edged sword
one side a sharp scalpel,
the other a dull rusty razor

it is a rose
velvety and smooth to the touch
but renowned for its thorns

also a patchwork quilt unraveling
pulling at the threads of community cohesion
leaving behind fiber fragmentation

very much a peacock festooned with vibrant feathers
visually appealing, yet masking
the less conspicuous displacement
and cultural shifts materializing beneath its epidermis

a rising tide,
that lifts a community's economic prospects
but often drowns its authentic, grassroots identity
beneath waves of upscale development

a two-faced coin
one side gleaming in "urban renewal"
the other casting long shadows
of displacement and erasure

an avalanche, a relentless rainstorm,
a hawk circling its prey,
a trapdoor spider,

a chameleon changing color
while flaunting its telltale swaying gait.

Johnnierenee Nia Nelson
Poet-Teacher, San Diego County

Pearls

Pearls are part of my memory
Not words about pearls or rhymes
not twisty-twirly puns, but real pearls
on necklaces and earrings and rings
on combs and pins
Perfectly round pearls and water pearls
that are odd-shaped lumpy things
Pearls that made a lover more real
not because he gave them to me
but because I wore them in his shine
Or I glowed a shine on a silver ring
that I hoped he would give
when I had bought it and said it was from him
Pearls part of love's imagining
Pearls on a tiara that just fit my 10 year old head
Pearls on a string that broke
My grandmother wrote a note
"Send to Tiffany, restring"
but there it was, still, bits and pieces,
almost lost, but not quite
Pearls on antique shoes, pearls someone dove for
Pearls in a box, scattered, found only in pictures in my mind
So valuable, yet only a thread-like thought holding it
Do these make me beautiful?
Or is it just a trick of sight
glinting as I glide through time
my own wonder being iridescent
perfect, round and off-white shining

Alice Pero
Poet-Teacher, Los Angeles County

Jackson's Nose

smells every green thing,
quivering nostrils,
each vibrates a different tune,
the left side classical,
right side Hip-Hop.

His body sways
to the blue road in between.
He doesn't mind
there's no sound in space.
The smells of chartreuse
enter his nose in octaves,
arpeggios, bumped by clef signs.

Birds add a riff,
black-brown root,
a gong of respect, humming.

He looks at wires in the sky
hears his voice repeated.
Space walking with Bach
worms watch from their squirming trail.

Cacophony laughing
at bent ears of wind
holding the symphony, instruments
of glee. Bee's, the back beat
of pollinating stories.

Jackson walks up to me, back-fires
his horn, laying down his track,
sprawling it over tuned keys,
notes of peaches, tuna,
and throaty meow.

Silence goes deep
below the high notes.

He is the bass, below bass,
the purple/black,
below music, below sound.

He flares both nostrils
making music.

Brian R. Martens
Poet-Teacher, Sonoma County

Breadth of Being

~ dedicated to the redwoods among us

Breathe in like trees do
swallow the dark, billowing plumes of asperity
exhale clear night air, owl-scattered skies
hands stretched across borders
breathe in dead decrees that serve few
breathe out freedom for all beings
families living in warm houses
drinking safe water
singing by a fire
grandparents reading to children
comfort your friend who wonders aloud
what she will do without her husband
bare her your dauntlessness
breathe in numb silence, breathe out a waterfall of tears
boat her down the river of permission

today, like yesterday and tomorrow
make soup, spiral, lift like black birds
breathe out long afternoons by the sea
light slanting toward dusk
breathe in storms, breathe out sun
sea mist, ghosts, sand castles
footsteps scrambling on rocks
breathe out summer, breathe in winter
climb inside every season
look around
discover where love loves you most
love it back as if your life depends on it
it does

breathe in broken shards of story
breathe out whole poems

Blake More
Poet-Teacher, Mendocino County

Dandelion Dictate

I'm not a wish for your child, the wishes for wings,
for princesses, play swords and kings.
I'm a wish for the moon, a wish for the sun.
A wish for twilight, for days that are done.
If wishes were kisses, I'd be very loved.
You can wish on a star or wish on a dove.
You think it's my whole globe that's a wish
but really each tuft is its own soon to be.
I offer you beauty, wonder and peace.
But for everything else, look for human guidance.
Please let my seeds loosen all on their own.
I ask to find my own way, let it be known.
You can wish on yourself. You must understand.
You can wish on each finger of each hand.
If you believe, as many children still can,
you can wish the world into healing again.
Don't worry your wishes, there isn't a cap.
And it makes sense if you wish for money and all that.
We need money to live, we need money to die.
That doesn't make sense, though. That doesn't make sense.
What do you wish for? For what do you want?
We all have the littles ones, we all have the longs.
And the hands of the children, the hands of the next,
the hands that are playing, the hands not yet vexed.
Please help them not need to wish for the world.
Let them still wish for a princess, a knight, a play sword,
wish for wings and mud puddles and everything warm.

Dawn Trook
Poet-Teacher, Merced County

To Paint a Thing of Beauty

To paint a thing of beauty
Start with a beak
Which sings sweet songs,
screeches warnings,
coos to attract a mate.
Next paint feathers of delight,
Scarlet head,
lemony body,
chartreuse neck.
Then paint a pair of wings
To ride the wind,
And migrate with the seasons.
To paint a thing of habit
born of greed, hate, and delusion,
start with an eleven pound head,
seeking to imprison
that which does not belong to it.
The head is indifferent to the suffering of others,
whether 189 caged parrots for sale,
or la gente
tortured and disappeared
by dictators.
Next paint two hands
with opposable thumbs
to grasp incessantly,
to possess
all that is beautiful and
vulnerable.
Then paint an insatiable belly
always craving,
never willing to share.
A thing of beauty is a joy forever,

it will continue to soar
while the one who soils its own nest,
locks others in poverty
will be left in ashes.

Lulu Wong
Poet-Teacher, Marin County

Spring Gifts

On the first sunny spring day
after a dark tumultuous winter
swarms of tiny lavender and white iris
dot the Mill Valley hills and trails
I hurry to drop off a late bill at the post office
where out front a young woman sits with baby
before a carboard tray of bracelets but I don't
slow down   head straight inside recalling
Ann Lamont's radio interview and
how she distributes bags of necessities
to the unhoused   takes time to sit and get
to know them   and as I hurry to my car
I find myself swerving to the back
flipping open the trunk for a few dollars
that I hand to the woman   saying,
It's just a donation   but she insists I take
a bracelet   so I look closer at tiny mock turquoise
beads skillfully strung with imitation gold
and an intricate twine clasp her grandmother wove
I can hardly make up my mind but finally
choose one, exactly the right minimal jewelry
for my older years and I'm smiling   as I drive
to Oakwood Trail   hurrying to finish my walk
when in front of me a tall elderly man hovers
above his grandson who is just barely
ambulatory   I slow my pace   patiently
follow baby's wobbling from one trail side
to the other   and when the path splits in two
I exclaim, *What a GOOD walker you are!*
and wide eyed   the toddler looks up   all smiles
answers with a shriek, then we chat in baby language
till he leans over unsteadily   and with great concentration

yanks out a large clump of grass   proudly hands it to me
Suddenly the day grows lovelier
leisurely   longer as I pause
wholeheartedly   receive this gift
then   carefully arrange
an altar on my dashboard
to bracelets and grass

Claire Blotter
Poet-Teacher, Marin County

A Miner's Lament

When I am not following the gold down,
into a maze of candlelit quartz walls and gunpowder
dead ends, it is following me, its glinty
footprints like crushed buttercup petals
scattered through the midnight meadows
of a Sierra foothills June, glowing in moonlight.
I only see the seasons on Sundays, a weekly chance to recognize
the depth of the snow, or witness the changes
in the maples, from buds to spring green, leaves that soon
dress themselves the color of fire, but all share a sad, brown finale,
in shapes like construction paper cut outs, falling
from a child's hands, to the forest floor.
Everything comes back to dirt.
From the depths of the mine, I crave
the blossoming, all the potential for new life
in sunlight, and yet, I am trapped. Like a sarcophagus
in an Egyptian tomb, surrounded by gilt gold, a captive
amid stale air and sealed passageways.
How can they be remembered, hidden
where no one is allowed—adorned in glorious
lapis and onyx boxes, with no one to admire their preciousness?
What purpose does gold serve after death?

And where does the gold that I find go?
Please spin it into thread for a quilter, embroider
my name onto the fabric of your memory. Weave it into a fine
filagree, adorn every finger on each of your hands, adjusting
the bands so that you can never take them off.

Hammer it into a polished chalice and carry me
to your lips. Grind it into powder and mix it with paint, illuminate
your manuscripts with my prayers of contrition, please
write, in gold ink, the divine story
of my losses.

                                                          Kirsten Casey
                                        Poet-Teacher, Nevada County

About California Poets in the Schools

Now in our 61th year, California Poets in the Schools has grown to become one of the oldest and largest writers-in-the-schools programs in the nation. Our reach includes 15,000 students served annually by 70 Poet-Teachers from throughout California. Poet-Teachers live and serve students K-12 in over 30 California counties, stretching from Humboldt and Siskiyou to Los Angeles and San Diego, in districts both urban and rural. Each year California Poets in the Schools' Poet-Teachers reach hundreds of classrooms, teaching in public and private schools, juvenile halls, after-school programs, hospitals and other community settings. California Poets in the Schools champions and amplifies the voices of California youth by providing platforms for critical literacy, youth development and leadership through school-based poetry writing, publication and performance opportunities.

California Poets in the Schools' vision is to enable youth in every California county to discover, cultivate and amplify their own creative voices through reading, analyzing, writing, performing and publishing poetry. When students learn to express their creativity, imagination, and intellectual curiosity through poetry, it becomes a catalyst for learning core academic subjects, accelerating emotional development and supporting personal growth. Poet-Teachers help students become adults who will bring compassion, understanding and appreciation for diverse perspectives both in and outside the classroom.

California Poets in the Schools develops and empowers a multicultural network of independent Poet-Teachers, who bring the many benefits of poetry to youth throughout the state. As a membership network we offer opportunities for professional development, peer learning and fundraising assistance for Poet-Teachers in California. We also cultivate relationships with school districts, foundations and arts organizations which can fund and support our members' professional practices.

Learn more at www.cpits.org
Contact us at info@cpits.org

Thank you to an anonymous donor, who believes strongly in our mission, for dedicating $5,000 to make this anthology possible. California Poets in the Schools is a 501(c)3 organization. Funding for this statewide anthology of youth poetry comes 100% from individuals and small businesses. We rely upon the generosity of the community to help us advance our mission and vision. A donation to our organization helps us to inspire more young people to find their unique voices through poetry, while expanding the audience for poetry.

Donate today at www.californiapoets.org.

www.ingramcontent.com/pod-product-compliance
Lightning Source LLC
Chambersburg PA
CBHW032036290426
44110CB00012B/834